MI STRATEGIES IN THE CLASSROOM AND BEYOND

Using Roundtable Learning

Ellen Weber, Ph.D.

MITA's International Brain-Based Renewal Center

Ken
To change and be changed!
Ellen

PEARSON
A and B

Boston ■ New York ■ San Francisco
Mexico City ■ Montreal ■ Toronto ■ London ■ Madrid ■ Munich ■ Paris
Hong Kong ■ Singapore ■ Tokyo ■ Cape Town ■ Sydney

Senior Editor: *Arnis E. Burvikovs*
Series Editorial Assistant: *Kelly Hopkins*
Marketing Manager: *Tara Whorf*
Production Administrator: *Annette Pagliaro*
Editorial Production: *Trinity Publishers Services*
Composition Buyer: *Linda Cox*
Manufacturing Buyer: *Andrew Turso*
Cover Administrator: *Kristina Mose-Libon*
Text Design and Composition: *Omegatype Typography, Inc.*

For related titles and support materials, visit our online catalog at www.ablongman.com.

Between the time Website information is gathered and then published, it is not unusual for some sites to have closed. Also, the transcription of URLs can result in unintended typographical errors. The publisher would appreciate notification where these errors occur so that they may be corrected in subsequent editions.

Library of Congress Cataloging-in-Publication Data

Weber, Ellen, 1946–
    MI strategies in the classroom and beyond : using roundtable learning / Ellen Weber.
        p. cm.
    Rev. ed. of: Roundtable learning. c1997.
    Includes bibliographical references and index.
    ISBN 0-205-40825-7 (pbk.)
    1. Learning, Psychology of—Case studies.   2. Multiple intelligences—Canada—Case studies.   3. Active learning—Canada—Case studies.   4. Group work in education—Canada—Case studies.   5. Lesson planning—Canada—Case studies.   6. Inuit—Education—Canada.   I. Title: Multiple intelligence strategies in the classroom and beyond.   II. Weber, Ellen, 1946– Roundtable learning.   III. Title.

LB1060.W43 2005
371.39—dc22

                                                                                2004050372

Printed in the United States of America

10   9   8   7   6   5   4   3   2   1   08   07   06   05   04

Contents

Preface

My reason initially for becoming a secondary school teacher and college professor was to help young people to reach more of their goals. For years, I focused on that motive in inner-city schools, high-performing public schools, and well-endowed private schools, where I met kids who appeared keen to get ahead and at times seemed hindered for one reason or another.

Even after many years, I still am fascinated to create and use new approaches to help learners discover their strengths in secondary school, college, and beyond. Equally fascinating to me is the privilege of collaborating with or supporting secondary and adult teachers who are eager to risk a change for the sake of learning more.

Whenever students feel they can connect to some concept in the classroom, they not only perform better in class, they are happier. The idea of helping young people to get ahead, in spite of the odds that hold some back, still inspires me. After more than thirty years in the field, I continue to find surprising insights about students, about myself, about other cultures, and about learning itself. This is perhaps why I still enjoy "going for gold." Students quickly get caught up in the excitement and build their own roundtables similar to those described in this book! On one occasion, we started a debate roundtable in a low-performing school. Students rose to the challenge and won the top debate championship that year. In speech classes, students who could hardly read found a way to excel with words in circles where they found something of interest to discover, develop, and teach to others in a safe but challenging setting.

In my first few years as a secondary school teacher, I became overwhelmed by the fact that many young people, and adults for that matter, seemed bored and disengaged by lectures. I realized that this boredom came from simply sitting and listening. I looked for answers, talked to learners and scholars from all over the world, and tried alternatives. Over time, this interest led me to research about the way our brains worked, and I used ideas from neuroscience to justify running off my lectures as handouts for students while we created together activities that they and I enjoyed more. It also led me to create roundtable approaches that engage and support teachers and to design them to be like a fireside chat. In these circles, we would start with teachers' best practices and build together for higher interest and achievement from that foundation. The roundtables described in this book factor in and value teacher strengths in the same way that teachers value their students' gifts. Roundtables take time to build consensus, which is why this work is less effective as a workshop or seminar, where argument or debate seems more prevalent than do application and alliance. While roundtables take time to build, change often comes quickly. However, I've found that change and risk taking gain support as people laugh and build scholarship opportunities and best practices together.

In many cases, the brain facts I illustrate and apply in this book have changed my own teaching, assessment, and team-building methods. Originally, I felt frustrated that ways to enhance brainpower are so hidden in medical terms that they do little to help teachers. I collaborated with others to change what I did as a teacher in an attempt to capitalize on students' unused mental resources. Students were as surprised as I was to discover the extravagant parts of their brains that remain dormant when they merely sit and listen or read to memorize for tests.

Within a few years, I grew convinced that when we work more with their brains, students work more with us. This idea revolutionized my classes, as it changed classes of secondary teachers and college faculty I taught at university. For this reason, when I taught lessons about another culture, I turned classrooms into a village square and conducted business in that culture. When I taught a new math concept, I turned the class into a bank for the day, and students became bank managers, employees, and clients. I enlisted them as experts on mock science boards and staged town meetings to speculate on government policy, clean up polluted rivers near their homes, and create learning systems that met real learning needs. Increasingly, students taught me that they care, they want to learn, and they can become motivated to view their own behavior in ways that will improve their chances for success. I found this to be the case even with students whose development lagged behind their peers.

Race, color, background, and beliefs seemed to melt away for my classes, as students came alive and valued the contributions of all in their roundtables. I discovered that students can learn to look beyond differences and to celebrate diverse perspectives when their own insights are valued. Brain-based insights defined and shared in this book led me to create richer roundtables that helped teachers and students to prosper. It seemed to me that when the right tone was established in my classes, students raced forward. Whenever they brought their interests to class in meaningful ways, we created a win-win situation for the whole group.

My doctoral dissertation focused on how teens bring many of what Howard Gardner called "multiple intelligences" to class. I created a teaching and assessment plan to use more of these as tools to learn and express knowledge in unique ways. This dissertation research translated into several books and many articles. As a result, I changed my own teaching and assessing to include more of what my students cared about and lived. One of the first differences I noticed was that extrinsic rewards were rarely needed to motivate students. Classroom management problems all but disappeared, even with more resistant students, when learning was linked to their lives.

Encouraged by the almost immediate response I found in higher motivation and higher grades attained, I carried related questions into the field of brain-based insights. Increasingly, I found myself asking *How can amazing new facts we learn daily about the human brain translate into new schools that capitalize more on human intelligence?* Now, each time I hear about a traditional teaching method that lets some students down, the more interested I become in how to spark their brains into learning again. This journey describes the original impetus for this book, and its daily adventures make me proud to be part of this profession.

In the race toward higher achievement in our schools and universities, we must take the time to stop, reflect, and consider our own beliefs about learning in order to make sure that what we believe is what we do in class. This book offers a set of beliefs linked to revolutionary facts now available about the human brain in the hope that this information will support improvements for secondary school and college classes. These pages are a reflection of what I learned myself from many students, master teachers, and mentors who converted brain-based facts into innovative practices that revolutionized their own roundtables.

As I write this preface, I reflect on thirty rewarding years during which students taught me more than I taught them. It has been a long and satisfying journey, and I am honored to have this opportunity to give back.

ACKNOWLEDGMENTS

Thanks to Robyn McMaster for kindness, inspiration, and generosity during our work together to create roundtables, both locally and internationally; to Arnis Burvikovs, for expertise, help, and encouragement during critical stages in the book's development; to Christine Lyons, for helping the book to launch; to Audrey Beth Stein, for stepping in at critical moments; and to Tara Whorf, for the energy she brings to this work at Allyn and Bacon.

Thanks to Howard Gardner, for inspiration and for taking risks for excellence; and to Thomas Hoerr, for applying brain-based work and nurturing excellence at New City School. Thanks to MITA leaders in Rochester, New York, and in Mexico, Canada, Australia, and Chile, where brain-based approaches are already shaping and being shaped in amazing roundtables!

Thanks to Tom and Dolores, for being there over a lifetime; and especially to my daughter, Tanya, for friendship and support during the book's creation. Thanks to Bev Still, Geoff Moore, Cindy Knott, and Reg Steward, for believing in this work and for excellence that spills from your care and talents into my life and work. To Faith and Ed Waters, Bruce Saulnier, Barbara Funk, Akosua Addo, and Keith LaSota—all leaders in the field to whom I look for wisdom and friendship.

Thanks also to the reviewers of the manuscript for their valuable suggestions: Elizabeth Aaronsohn, Central Connecticut State University; Rick Gay, Davidson College; Tom Hoerr, New City School; Ann Mitchell, Greece Central School District; Michelle Scribner-MacLean, University of Massachusetts–Lowell; Karl Thielking, Pittsford–Mendon High School; Dianne V'Marie, University of Phoenix Online.

I owe deepest appreciation to the community of learners with whom I am privileged to work year after year. These are the students, parents, and teachers who refresh me with their expertise, scholarship, and honest contributions to this profession. Because of you the field has been more than good to me over a lifetime.

About the Author

Ellen Weber, Ph.D., has lived and worked among cultures as far north as the high Arctic and as far south as Chile. She has taught brain-based approaches to students, faculty, and leaders in world-class universities. Dr. Weber asks the question "How are your students smart, and how can you tell?" A leader's leader, she provides dozens of samples to show how faculty and students can raise test scores and enjoy learning. Weber's five-step brain-based program in this book leads students to higher motivation and achievement at secondary school and college levels.

Weber is principal and CEO of MITA's International Brain-Based Renewal Center in Rochester, New York. Weber's brain-based books on MITA learning and assessment provide dozens of practical examples of Brain-Friendly Strategies, for increased motivation and higher student achievement. The MITA Renewal Program—*Five Steps to Smart*—described in this book is used to renew curriculum in secondary schools and colleges within several countries. Experts at the brain-based center welcome opportunities to discuss innovative possibilities for secondary and college faculty's professional development.

MITA Renewal Program Website: http://www.mitaleadership.com

Ellen Weber can be reached at eweber1@frontiernet.net

Introduction

The mind is capable of anything—because everything is in it, all the past as well as all the future.

Joseph Conrad, *Heart of Darkness*

Can you imagine a learning environment that showcases every student's gifts, abilities, and interests? Visualize a place where teens love to come, where ideas brim over, and where the elderly enjoy sharing stories with youth in order to illustrate wisdom they have accumulated over the years. Picture a circle where gifted students and experts-to-be take risks to teach each other as they learn from one another and where all feel valued. Imagine a room where every person who enters is considered unique in some way, and you will see a metaphorical crown held over each learner's head.

This book provides strategies to build unique environments so that secondary or college students want to be there and will learn and prosper. The basis of this book is roundtable learning. Roundtable approaches differ from teacher-centered classrooms in that learners become a valued part of an interactive exchange among people of various ages, cultures, and walks of life. Each participant, including the teacher, is both teacher and student. One key curriculum question or one central problem to be solved creates the community's core agenda, and assessment tasks double as learning tools.

THE ROUNDTABLE PROCESS

The roundtable process described in these pages sets the stage for a learning process characterized by challenge and satisfaction. William Yeats described a similar successful approach by building on students' strengths when he stated, "Learning is more the lighting of a fire than the filling of a pail." For Dewey, students' inner "fires" were ignited through active learning, which he described as a process that involved discovery and delightful curiosity. Students activate their unique capability to learn when we help them to create.

I remember a few years ago when, after many years of teaching high school and college, I identified with Los, a character in Blake's poem "Jerusalem." Los said: "I must Create a System, Or be enslav'd by another Man's (human's). I will not Reason or Compare, My business is to Create." Los probably speaks to many teachers today who work tirelessly to make their classrooms reflect new understandings about how the brain works and how their students learn in brain-compatible environments. We cannot wait for the status quo to improve. Improvement comes through the efforts of one teacher at a time and one student at a time. This book supports and applauds those teachers who risk lighting new fires in their students. Whenever faculty build classroom communities in which students actively construct new meanings, they create renewal. Knowledge in these roundtable circles adds value to understanding through inquiry, self-reflection, collaborative learning, problem solving, and integration of skills and ideas. Ideas formerly lost in one-method-only approaches or taught in one-time-only workshops require follow-up. Change waits in the wings for support.

The roundtable teaching design provides an ongoing support system that can generate learning circles in which faculty help and are helped. Based on the MITA (multiple intelligences theory to achievement) model (Weber, 1995), roundtable teaching invites people to lead with their strengths and to achieve excellence. This approach views all students as "gifted." These gifts come alive in MITA classes. Both faculty and students learn to stir a sense of wonder for each new topic. Quality learning follows when students draw on their past experiences, their faith, their worldview, and their unique talents, as tools for deeper understanding. Teachers who light fires will celebrate new ideas in any learning community. The converse is also true. When teachers ignore students' personal unique learning preferences, or insist on one approach only, they tend to hinder genuine progress.

This book has two main purposes. First, it provides practical, hands-on classroom activities and lesson plan suggestions. Lessons are brain based, in that they integrate best practices from brain-compatible learning theories such as multiple intelligences, inquiry-based learning, problem-based approaches, reflective thinking, differentiated instruction, state standards, and authentic assessments. Second, each chapter emphasizes lessons that will access your students' brainpower in new ways. These lessons are related to a current learning theory through practical *Five Steps to Smart* strategies. Throughout the book, you will integrate practices and theories you may have heard about or studied but have not used with your students. In addition, this program will draw on your own best practices. The suggestions made here will offer you new ways to *question* possibilities, *target* improvements, *expect* quality, *move* resources, and *reflect* on growth possibilities to integrate brain-based activities into your classes.

In order to help you to integrate ideas and practices, the book outlines three umbrella approaches. You are invited to reshape and use lessons to match the needs of your own classes. In the process, you can expect to exchange some of your traditional ideas and keep others. You may lecture less or teach from fewer practice tests in exchange for new insights and active learning approaches. You may want to keep some of your traditional approaches as long as they act to propel your students beyond the requirements for any standardized test. What you keep or exchange may differ from class to class.

VYGOTSKY'S LEARNING THEORY

Learning, according to Lev Vygotsky (1986), is a social process, and students advance by teaching others as they learn themselves. Vygotsky showed evidence for a classroom where students teach and learn from one another in both traditional and renewed ways. In other words, students learn in community and through team building, as well as through student-led conferences in which novices teach experts and experts at times assume the roles of novices. In roundtable approaches, experts with more skill and experience support novices, and novices feel secure taking the risks required to grow. Even in community, learning is highly individual. For one task, certain students rise to expert levels; for other tasks, they learn from peers. This fact was illustrated to me when I visited a secondary school where Robyn McMaster, senior vice-president at the MITA Renewal Center, was conducting a student-led conference to interpret literature through digital videos. In one group, a student named Brad had created a video that interpreted one text through artistic ability. Brad had to read the chapters many times to understand the themes. Since the team valued Brad's ability to apply technology and create Internet connections, they helped him to understand the text. Because of this teamwork, the group earned a near-perfect score on the project.

For Vygotsky, students do not learn by passing through similar sets of stages as a class or group. In fact, Brad failed most essays in his junior year. Then he began to build on his strengths, such as his understanding of technology, in team settings. For Brad and for most students, learning within a community requires access to each person's prior knowledge and prior experience. You will find tasks such as interest inventories in this book to enable you to collect, file, and retrieve ideas about students like Brad that will help all of your learners connect to and benefit from the lessons you teach.

Vygotsky opposed those who held that teaching is less effective with older students. He taught that development occurs spontaneously and is affected by how and what one is taught, regardless of age. Vygotsky's views are reflected here in the emphasis on teachers as sensitive, responsive facilitators of knowledge rather than as deliverers of facts. His influence also underlies the focus on tasks that stimulate students' minds and imaginations to come to life in new ways as they learn. Vygotsky claimed that learning improves whenever students can look back at their development and understand future possibilities. This view supports the integration design of this text.

This book is rooted in Vygotsky's notion of all learning as a socially derived development. Activities are provided in each chapter that help students shift from needing the help of others into more self-regulation as they work together with others. This is rooted in Vygotsky's zone of proximal development, typically defined as the space between getting help to solve problems and independent performances that follow capable guidance from adults or capable peers. The book builds lessons in ways that Vygotsky described as meaningful interpersonal interactions. He challenged teachers to step back from talking in order to engage all students actively. This goal forms a significant part of the book's intent to provide practical ways to do just that in upper-level classes.

As we engage our students' past, build on their talents, and leverage interactions within learning communities, we motivate students to develop stronger abilities. When we encourage students to apply their strengths in order to learn new lessons, we strengthen their whole community. Following Vygotsky's principles, students teach one another at the same time as they learn themselves. Activities in this book show how to build vibrant classroom communities through shared experiences and unleashed talents.

GARDNER'S MULTIPLE INTELLIGENCES

Howard Gardner has been called one of the brightest minds of our times. Gardner offers research to support assessments and learning tasks that engage the more natural intelligences that students bring to every topic they encounter. His work has inspired my own over many areas and is a main foundation for all applications found in this book. His encouragement has motivated me into an exciting intellectual adventure, and his path-breaking developments and observations about the measures and meanings of intelligence underscore most of the work I do to convert insights about intelligence into successful performances in secondary and college classes. According to Gardner, humans possess many ways of knowing and expressing their worlds. This book shows what this idea looks like when learners use it to capitalize on their unique strengths.

Gardner identifies eight distinct intelligences and suggests these are developed and expressed in specific tasks within each discipline. Unlike learning styles, which express student preferences for learning in one way or another, such multiple intelligences exist within each student, in varying degrees.

A summary of Gardener's eight ways of knowing follows:

- **Mathematical-logical** intelligence includes scientific or mathematical ability, the capacity to discern logical or numerical patterns, and the ability to handle long chains of reasoning.

- **Verbal-linguistic** intelligence includes speaking; poetic or journalistic ability; sensitivity to the sounds, rhythms, and meanings of words; and understanding the various functions of language.

- **Musical-rhythmic** intelligence includes the ability to compose music and play an instrument; the ability to produce and appreciate rhythm, pitch, and timbre; and the appreciation of various forms of musical expressiveness.

- **Visual-spatial** intelligence includes navigator's and sculptor's abilities and the capacity to perceive the visual-spatial world accurately.

- **Bodily-kinesthetic** intelligence includes the ability to dance and engage in athletics, the ability to control one's body movements, and the ability to handle objects skillfully.

- **Interpersonal** intelligence includes the capacity to discern and respond appropriately to the moods, temperaments, motivations, and desires of other people.

- **Intrapersonal** intelligence includes accurate self-knowledge, access to one's feelings and the ability to discriminate among them, and the ability to draw on one's feelings to direct behavior.

- **Naturalistic** intelligence includes an ability to draw on patterns and designs in nature in order to solve real-world problems.

Emotional intelligence, which is included in the intrapersonal domain, provides students and faculty with an ability to understand and use their intelligences as tools for learning. Along with Howard Gardner, Daniel Goleman (1995) has made us more aware that emotions are too often ignored in current classes. In his book *Emotional Intelligence,* Goleman shows the need to recognize strengths and weaknesses in one's emotions in order to regulate feelings, understand and work with others' emotions, and show empathy for others. In this book, you will find intrapersonal intelligence described in ways that enhance both cognitive and emotional intelligence as a way to promote learning. The main emphasis is on practical approaches that suggest the importance of emotional intelligence and then offer ways that it can be better developed in a class. This involves particular skills provided to help students develop the ability to motivate themselves, regulate their moods, control impulses, and empathize with others.

WEBER'S FIVE-STEP PLAN

After much research and after working among several cultures, I introduced a practical five-step-strategy plan to demonstrate how students learn through engaging their strengths, both individually and in collaboration with others. Over many years, I worked alongside some faculty who adhered more to theory as well as others who emphasized improved practical approaches to learning. It seemed to me that one gap in this spectrum was the integrated mix between solid theory and active student learning at its best.

This recognition underscores my own work, which includes an integration of theory with the renewed practice that emanates from it. Rather than separate brain-related information into a separate chapter, I chose to integrate this material into chapters that describe practices that encourage using facts in practical ways to refresh a class. I have integrated stories about Inuit teachers and others with whom I worked in the hope these will provide ideas and inspiration for your work.

My MITA program is steeped in current theories about the mind and about learning but also provides practical ideas for creating vibrant roundtable learning environments by affirming what teachers and students do well and by bringing together best practices from many research sources as well as from diverse cultures. While the practical program described in this book is original, at the same time it is also derived from brain-based ideas that master teachers had put forward long before neuroscience affirmed their worth. This book is an integrated mix of theories that leads to higher achievement and motivation, especially at the secondary school and university levels. This book supports doable methods that help teachers to develop and capitalize on resources their students already possess but perhaps fail to use in class. Many people have inspired me to help students to achieve new accomplishments by using parts of their brains never before used. It is my hope that faculty and students will find the magic I have found in this endeavor. Just as my own research starts with questions, so can your exploration start with questions pertinent to what you teach and how you assess, such as "What's the single most important thing you can do to unleash within your students to open up a new view of some provocative idea or authentic wisdom?" or "How has theory made your classes encouraging or inspiring as the inner workings of great minds?"

This book will spur such questions about your teaching, acting as a conduit that links excellent practices in the classroom, beyond the dry scholarship of the academic world, to expand students' minds for higher standards. Figure 0.1 shows five brain-based traits that lead to growth. The opposite of growth for each trait is also shown so that teachers can determine where the growth areas lie. By pinpointing one specific area of growth potential in your learning community, you will gain more value from the MITA lessons in the chapters that follow.

What does your classroom look like, and what barriers do you face? Figure 0.2 shows traits that exist in brain-based classes. Look for these traits, which are already evident in your students, and identify other traits that you would like to see developed as you apply suggestions from this book.

You may wish to start by identifying barriers that hold your students back from higher motivation and achievement. Figure 0.3 shows two barriers that can obstruct your students. Expect to replace barriers with brain-based opportunities as you work through the lessons in the next few chapters.

Where do you see your students in relation to MITA's growth?

Question + Target + Expect + Move + Reflect = Growth

_____ + Target + Expect + Move + Reflect = Passivity

Question + _____ + Expect + Move + Reflect = Confusion

Question + Target + _____ + Move + Reflect = Sloppiness

Question + Target + Expect + _____ + Reflect = Waste

Question + Target + Expect + Move + _____ = Stagnation

The MITA Program guides teachers and students to higher motivation and achievement. Opposite results to MITA growth steps include: passivity, confusion, sloppiness, wasted talent, or stagnation.

Question
possibilities

When students begin their lessons with a **question**, the mind shifts from passive to active. Their brain launches new pathways toward new possibilities in response.

Target
improvements

The brain will **target** specific goals in order to avoid confusion. When students see targets as a flag on a mountain peak, the brain finds motivation to reach that peak, and learning improves.

Expect
quality

To **expect** quality is to create detailed checklists of best qualities for the brain to create. These traits include size, shapes, colors, textures, and functions that show the details sought in a project.

Move
resources

To **move**, students actively create knowledge through Gardner's multiple intelligences, and through their mental resources. Students select parallel pathways to high standards, and often lead with their strengths to reach improved outcomes.

Reflect
on growth possibilities

To **reflect** is to revisit the finished work in order to adjust for future growth. At this phase students are encouraged to ask, "Where to from here?" and to develop an action plan with growth possibilities.

FIGURE 0.1
MITA Model for *Five Steps to Smart* Program

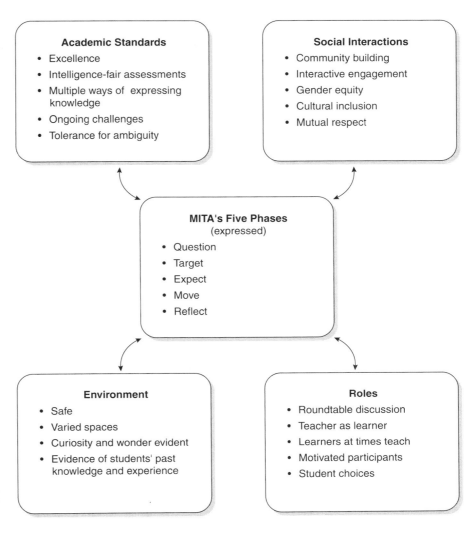

FIGURE 0.2
Traits That Describe a
Successful Brain-Based
Class

The MITA model suggests three C's for brain-based learning:

1. **Collaboration** implies teamwork among teachers, parents, and students. The MITA model describes how joint efforts are set up and suggests an approach for initiating effective communication. (The model outlined in this book is described in further detail in Weber, 1999.) Open new doors for meaningful exchanges across disciplines so that integration of excellent ideas emerges as partnerships grow.

2. **Content** includes brainstorming with students, ideas from Gardner's multiple intelligences theory, interest inventories to ascertain students' unique intelligences, and integrated curriculum tasks.

3. **Criteria** include suggestions and rubrics for negotiating assessment and for presenting and videotaping projects. In the roundtable process, assessment is part of the overall learning process, contrary to the tests and quizzes that form separate entities at the end of each unit in traditional lessons.

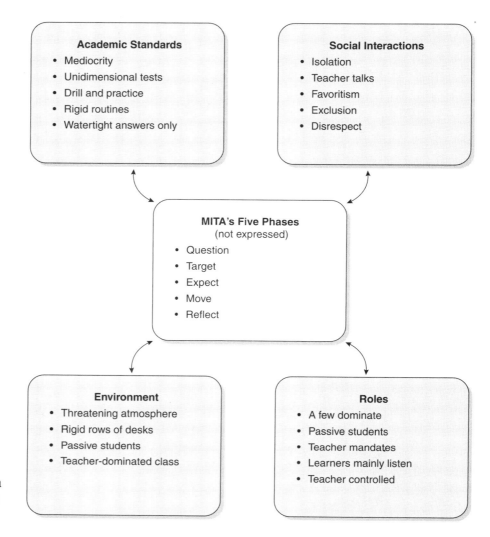

FIGURE 0.3
Barriers That Impede a Brain-Based Approach to Class

BRIDGING GAPS BETWEEN RESEARCH AND PRACTICE

In this book, you'll construct practical bridges between research theory and classroom practices in order to increase motivation and achievement for secondary and college students. Some questions teachers might ask are

"How does a person construct new knowledge using past insights and past experiences as a positive foundation?"

"How can multiple intelligences bring positive results in my discipline?"

"How do we acquire ways of thinking and acting that make up a community's culture?"

"How do we optimize cooperative dialogues and activities with knowledgeable members of any community?"

By asking such questions, faculty examine ways to create social interactions that foster active learning and begin to create strong learning environments within high school and university classrooms. Some elementary schools have created social learning contexts over the past several years, but higher education has lagged behind. This is owing partly to a lack of practical tools and partly because some activities are not linked to learning experiences or lesson objectives. Activities throughout this book provide roundtable learning practices that improve motivation and achievement in a step-by-step plan. The hands-on activities will reveal how community settings act as conduits for fostering social relationships that develop unique, culturally adaptive competencies. We are an increasingly pluralistic society, and growth comes from harnessing the strengths from diverse groups. When faculty capitalize on strengths from within a variety of cultures, they also foster quality learning in their own classrooms.

Most teachers would agree that learning is an active process requiring participation in social dialogues that surround culturally important tasks. Depending on a person's cultural experiences, different societies generate different skills. For example, the Inuit in the Arctic are required to travel and hunt to survive. Such cultural demands require elaborate spatial and kinesthetic skills. In the fierce blizzards that relentlessly pound the harsh Arctic tundra, the Inuit hunter travels with what one elder described as only "a compass in his head." All students can learn from the skills that the Inuit value, and so it is with skills possessed by each student and culture represented in a class. The key is to find a way to optimize students' abilities and relate their strengths to each topic. This can be done in brain-based roundtables, which are modeled and illustrated in each chapter of the book.

FIGURE 0.4 MITA's *Five Steps to Smart*

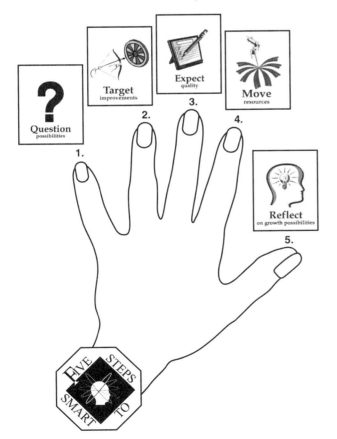

This book is loosely organized into three larger sections based on major components of roundtable learning. Chapters 1 through 2 define brain-based interactions and suggest activities to create one shared question for each lesson topic. Chapters 3 through 5 outline strategies to identify all students' unique gifts and highlight motivational activities to maximize those gifts. Chapters 6 through 7 redefine mistakes as stepping stones to deeper understandings, rather than as errors to be highlighted by a red x in the margin of students' work.

The classroom activities included in this book come out of years of working with teachers, students, and parents and the exchange of activities that helps increase interest and enhance quality learning in classrooms. I have used many of these activities in seminars, TV programs, and even in high school or college online classrooms. I constantly test these exercises in schools where I facilitate faculty to create brain-compatible roundtables. The concept of roundtable learning and the activities included here represent a grassroots movement among diverse colleagues who exchange good ideas, demonstrate excellent learning approaches, and create a love of learning among their students.

Figure 0.4 shows five triggers to activate more brainpower from students. Look for some or all of these in the following chapters, and you will help bring out and develop students' unused or hidden intelligences.

In brain-based practices, where teachers integrate theories and practices that include new facts about the human brain and where practices reflect that integration, you will see the connections in action illustrated in Figure 0.5.

Many of the insights in these chapters came from students who attended MITA roundtables and who taught me about how to teach secondary and college classes effectively using a roundtable rather than a lecture approach. Building on what your students already do well, or what you have observed through workshops and seminars, you can apply roundtable methods to help your students absorb more information by uncovering insights themselves and making these ideas their own tools for life in and beyond their classes.

FIGURE 0.5 Your Beliefs Shape Your Outcomes

If you believe that . . .	*Then you will want to . . .*
teacher talk does not equate to student learning.	convert lectures into handout resources for students' investigation.
creative people inspire great end results.	start to motivate creativity in all students.
mistakes are stepping stones for excellence.	help students risk whatever it takes to improve.
students can be guided into higher achievement.	convert assessment tasks into learning tools.
today's realities may not contain tomorrow's best practices.	challenge and test traditions to add more appropriate approaches.
students are the highest currency of any classroom.	expect and welcome students' best, brightest, and most creative ideas.
students can accomplish what they have never before accomplished.	help students to use parts of their brains never before used.
all students can reach higher standards.	change what you do daily to improve goals.
curiosity can increase students' aptitude to learn.	ask two-footed questions so that one foot links to students' interests and one foot links to core content you expect them to learn.
lifelong learning is the opposite of cynicism and pessimism.	adopt the motto: We can change things together. We can be the best!
it works to "go with your gut."	do not take action if you sense a 40% chance of being right, but don't wait until you are 100% sure.
encouragement does more than criticism to nurture students at all achievement levels.	create a caring culture where students sense a positive response to their ideas and where they expect to achieve excellence.
diversity can help all students to contribute more.	encourage all students to learn and teach interactively.
learning can be fun.	call on imagination as Einstein did when he pictured himself riding the curve of the arc.
change can be lonely.	accept the fact that some will criticize.
others will support your best ideas.	surround yourself with those who believe in and use best practices.

CHAPTER 1

Roundtable Learning Creates Vibrant Communities

Wisdom is not a product of schooling but of the lifelong attempt to acquire it.

Albert Einstein

LESSONS FROM AN INUIT COMMUNITY

Through many generations, Inuit communities have used circle gatherings to solve practical problems, respond to cultural issues, explore new ideas, and heal relationships. In much the same way that learning circles operate in Inuit classrooms and communities, I've used circles to enhance learning in secondary and college classrooms. For two years, I lived far north of the Arctic Circle. I learned from many Inuit colleagues and friends how circles help students to solve problems collaboratively, because many problems are especially hard to unravel alone. This chapter illustrates roundtable configurations that bring together brain-based learning practices that faculty already use so that every student can succeed, as in the case of Jason.

Jason told his circle how he hated to write because he didn't know where to start. After a circle discussion, in which Jason excelled in comments and insights about every topic the group raised and in which his peers shared similar problems, Jason said he felt "less stupid." Jason had difficulty extracting meaning from sentences, and his impairment had grown worse over years of failure to the point where he defined himself by his flawed attempts to express meaningful ideas on paper. But Jason had paid careful attention to how others organized and presented their thoughts, and he began to approach his writing assignments in the creative ways he had discovered as the group brainstormed together. This led to feelings of success for Jason.

In learning communities, students like Jason can find the space to discover and use their strengths. The best circles are much like the castle illustrated in Figure 1.1. In each tower of their minds, students can view and express facts from a unique framework. They can also learn from one another's perspectives and integrate the best learning methods.

In Baffin Island's northern communities, I witnessed circles that enabled teachers and students to solve complex academic problems with increased understanding. When I used similar circles in secondary and college classes, students like Jason welcomed collaborative opportunities to explore issues in new ways. When facilitated well, the roundtable approach supports the following new directions:

- Two-footed questions address students' interests and abilities as well as learning expectations from the content. These questions provide opportunities for students to probe content more deeply and also engage students' interests and abilities

- Talents become personal tools for learning.

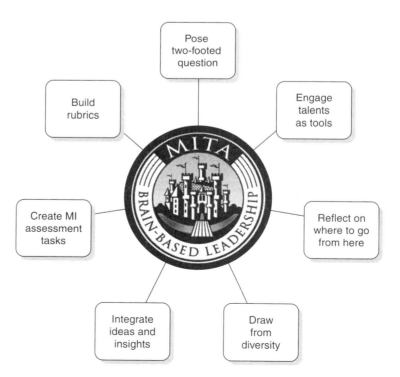

FIGURE 1.1
Integration Is Key to
Roundtable Learning

- Students pause to reflect together in order to ensure ongoing growth.

- Diversity becomes a rich storehouse, providing insights from different perspectives.

- Ideas and solutions come from various disciplines and learning approaches.

- Multiple intelligences motivate all students, and alternative assessments are the result.

- Rubrics provide clear, parallel pathways and benchmarks to higher standards.

Imagine students standing in each tower and looking through the windows at the scenes outside. As they view a topic from one tower, they see angles and opportunities not visible from another. Brain-based learning allows students to move from tower to tower so that they can see facts from alternative viewpoints. In fact, this castle illustration suggests a metaphor for avoiding the mental passivity fostered by too many lectures.

Figure 1.2 shows the degrees to which retention levels are typically higher whenever students use more of their brains to learn. Because the circle approach opens new opportunities for learners to use active brain-based tactics (which are discussed in depth throughout this book), it also creates prospects for deeper understanding. Students enjoy both the space to use their individual abilities and the opportunity to develop relationships that help team growth. From a brain-based standpoint, the reasons for higher achievement are clear. When students attempt to retrieve facts and apply ideas in standardized tests, they revisit their viewpoints mentally and remember interactions from several "castle towers," and so their answers reflect these different angles.

Research suggests that when students learn in this way, and when expectations are high, students do better. Even in instances in which standardized tests assess knowledge from one or two intelligences only, students begin to lead with their strengths. In this way, they shore up weaker areas. A student who writes less well becomes motivated to express keen ideas. One who lacks comprehension abilities in one learning approach gains ground in another. Jason, for instance, represents many students who do well when they can lead with their unique mix of strengths. In a well-formed circle, students with difficulties in some areas build strong alliances with others who do well in these areas. But in the circle, students hold each other accountable for areas in which they excel.

Disengaged students in high school and college seemed to leap onboard when faculty replace lectures with circles as problem-solving devices. Higher-achieving students also benefit by finding opportunities to explore new angles, creating products that reflect higher thinking skills, and teaching others as they learn themselves. In fact, test scores tend to climb for almost all the students whenever they participate in circles in which learners are encouraged to teach and teachers also can learn.

Several circles I observed in Inuit communities generated different perspectives and provided more practical applications of current theories than rote

FIGURE 1.2 Using Brain Capabilities

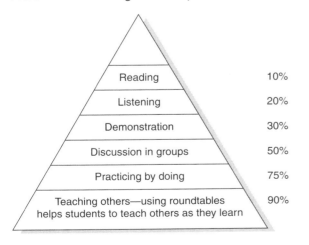

Reading	10%
Listening	20%
Demonstration	30%
Discussion in groups	50%
Practicing by doing	75%
Teaching others—using roundtables helps students to teach others as they learn	90%

memory or emphasis on one approach only. In the following ways, discovery becomes the handmaiden of best practices for more students:

- Inquiry-based learning becomes two-footed questions; students find motivation and teachers target higher standards.

- Problem-solving methods beg new solutions; students create innovative explanations and even re-create wheels in unique ways.

- Authentic assessments set the stage for projects that relate to real-life issues and to communities beyond the classroom.

- Students bring their unique mix of intelligences to the circle as tools to understand and apply new ideas for each topic introduced.

Not surprisingly, such interactive learning forums enable vibrant communities that include many cultures. Some call this differentiated learning. The Education Commission of the States report *Future Trends Affecting Education* (www.ecs.org/clearinghouse/13/27/1327.htm) predicts that a much higher emphasis will be placed on highly personalized learning, student achievement, accountability, and school choice.

In roundtables, students benefit from solutions that arise from diverse backgrounds and experiences. They are held accountable for and reap many benefits associated with their own and with each participant's unique contributions. Research suggests that school choice is closely related to new needs and new curricula that will emerge when we help students to sift through methods that bring higher motivation and higher achievement into their worlds.

Faculty commonly agree that in the best roundtables or brain-compatible settings, more students find freedom to make mistakes and gather courage to take risks. Learners no longer sit quietly as passive recipients of the teacher's knowledge; instead, they assume the role of active participants in their own growth. Effective roundtables can actually alter the chemical and electrical activity within the human brain such that students can learn more because their brains are nurtured in the learning process. Some faculty may not be aware that chemical changes in students' brains can be initiated by the formations and expectations within the classroom community. Faculty and students together can instigate positive changes through brain-compatible circles that enable students to benefit more from their classes.

Throughout each chapter, you'll find facts about your students' brains including multiple intelligences and electrical and chemical functioning in the brain that can speed up or slow down learning. This information is integrated into conversations, as in a fireside chat in which faculty consider how their roundtables might take advantage of brain-based learning. The theme of roundtables provides a unifying factor for this book. I do not intend this to be a text in neuroscience. I've drawn from several fields and present here a practical integration of learning practices in order to stretch the mission of learning beyond any one field or theory and to show the wonder of students' mental capabilities.

In brain-compatible circles, students' brains release more serotonin, a hormone that creates a sense of well-being, thereby allowing them to take risks without fear of recrimination. In contrast, cortisol, a hormone creating a sense of unease, spills into the brain whenever fear or uncertainty characterizes learning. Without fear of failure or the uncertainty that increases cortisol and shuts down learning, students of many cultures take risks to understand the most complex topics. In teacher-dominated classes, some students tend to remain quiet or allow only one dominant culture's perspectives to emerge. In contrast, brain-compatible settings foster contributions from diverse individuals.

While well-being is a critical component of learning, it does not necessarily mean ease or comfort. In fact, small doses of cortisol may be necessary at times and may help initiate a rush of adrenaline that can nudge some students toward higher achievement on certain tests. The key is to challenge and engage students without diminishing or shortchanging them. To do this, faculty can create safe and, at the same time, challenging circles using what I have termed *two-footed questions.*

TWO-FOOTED QUESTIONS

In roundtables, the best questions become two footed, so that one foot points to students' interests and abilities and the other foot steps into the lesson topic. Each prong of two-footed questions increases curiosity to learn more about a topic, and each moves thinking along toward a doable resolution. For example, a teacher might ask, *What happened in the Civil War that affects you and your family?* Or in math class, a two-footed question might be, *How might these graphs influence your life today?* A science question that is two footed may ask, *What lives in the river near you?* Or in English, the question could be *If you were Pablo Neruda, what poem would you write about your government's role in Iraq?* This harmonious learning environment motivates students of all ages and propels new ideas, as people feel validated to use their unique abilities in concert with others to orchestrate knowledge that impacts life as they know it.

Whenever faculty ask questions that disregard students' interests and abilities, they disconnect their learning goals from their students' motivation to achieve these goals. For example, if one asks "What happened during the Civil War?" many students will reply "I don't care." If however, faculty disregard the foot that probes their content areas deeply, they decrease many students' chances for successful achievement. For example, ask, "How do you feel about the Civil War?" and students will cascade their emotions and ideas without much attention to historic facts. If, on the other hand, you ask, "What happened in the Civil War that affects you and your family today?" you bring a sense of immediacy and meaning to the topic. In so doing, you create a brain-compatible opportunity that engages students, who will then use their talents as tools to discover deeper understanding. At the same time they will apply new insights to their current situations and will relate what they learn to similar events they encounter in their own worlds.

Faculty that I facilitate or work alongside of in roundtable projects often discuss how they achieve successful learning circles in a variety of difficult settings. At times, they experience barriers we all face, and they note how these obstacles hold students back at one time or another. Then they look for ways to move past learning barriers in order to achieve creative opportunities. Barriers for these teachers, and for most of us, often seem surprisingly similar, and yet teachers too often face isolation as they try to move beyond their particular blockades.

Resistant students, pressures from parents, too much text to cover, and high-stakes-tests demands often top their expressed list of difficulties. In fact, round-tables are ideal settings for presenting for discussion the most difficult barriers so that faculty can find and share real solutions. In the pages that follow, you will find several guides to creating your own best solutions, regardless of the topics you teach.

Following eighteen months of working with and learning from Inuit teachers, I piloted several new programs that applied successful roundtable learning activities and teaching strategies. Whenever I introduce roundtable learning approaches within a variety of ages, people ask how it is possible to work with so many different entry points. Circles tend to work best when they integrate a variety of different ages, interests, and abilities. At their core, roundtables enhance interactions in formal classroom settings as well as in more active classrooms, where students are used to learning alone as well as in teams. Whether on campus or online, round-table learning presupposes inquiry as a collaborative process.

Following are some Websites that can enhance meaningful two-footed questions in your classes.

1. http://sll.stanford.edu/projects/tomprof/newtomprof/postings/175.html
   This site illustrates questions that will guide students to deeper understanding on any topic.

2. http://www.newhorizons.org/
   This site illustrates lessons plans and strategies for building community and promoting learning for secondary students.

CREATING A TONE THAT NURTURES THOUGHT

Students enjoy an opportunity to create positive communities where new ideas are evoked and where they can take time to look at facts through the eyes of others. This section includes a list of criteria that can be used to guide a secondary or college class to foster safe and yet challenging circles. Using the list of criteria below, have students create quotes that describe their groups' mission for a positive learning climate. Each quote should encourage all students to find opportunities in the roundtables in order to express their ideas and relate these to new facts learned. You can display the quotes on a large poster or bulletin board as daily guides to

- feel free to express their minds, in respect and without any attack in response

- expect the best from others concerning topics raised, but also to accept imperfections

- contribute freely to ideas and feel valued in small teams and in class

- look forward to engaging peers in thoughtful ways for diverse responses

- show positive attitudes to others' different ideas, even when they disagree

- state specific supports that agree or disagree with issues raised in class

- apologize whenever offense is taken by any member of the group

- think deeply and then state ideas so that others can learn from them

- laugh at themselves and shake off personal offenses when they come

FIGURE 1.3 Tone Lights the Way
for Circle Strengths

- maintain a careful tone that affirms people and leads with creative ideas

- learn skills to report insights so that others benefit from the solutions

- take the risk to lead, and gain the humility to be led by others in the group

You may also wish to create your own criteria to reverse a negative climate in a circle and build a stronger learning community in your class. Nothing can substitute for a good climate, and it takes an entire team to create and sustain the positive qualities that promote success for the entire group.

Sarcasm and debate for the sake of argument only are not helpful in this process, as they tend to shut out voices that might otherwise be heard. Creating the best circles takes skill and a daily resolve to build positive contributions. In fact, building the tone of the circle is a daily endeavor, one that lights warm flames and inspires higher visions for the team. (See Figure 1.3.)

COLLABORATION AMONG STUDENTS, TEACHERS, AND COMMUNITY

Faculty who learn alongside their students and who guide discussions, facilitate problem solving, and instigate reflection encourage interactive learning at its best. They create dynamic inquiry beyond mandated agendas set by boards or imposed by outside forces. Ideas spring into life from many perspectives. The best of these ideas remain after being filtered through the group's sieve of common understanding and shared vision.

When I taught on Baffin Island, Inuit students' and teachers' personal and traditional stories created course content that encompassed Inuit culture and heritage. Eventually, we compiled students' stories into a text for our social studies course. Stories we had shared in our talking circles provided our supplemental information for such lessons as "How Do Inuit Children Learn Best?" The idea was to integrate traditional Inuit knowledge into the required McGill course outline. The students' personal experiences in Arctic living were added to their course content. Teamwork was based on the following assumption about learning: *Just as we hinder learning whenever we ignore a culture's unique past knowledge and experiences, so do we move toward shared outcomes when we include students' past knowledge at the most basic levels.*

Traditional Inuit stories proved to be relevant, participatory, and inquiry driven. Motivation grew for each lesson as students talked to elders, collaborated with one another, and interviewed former teachers. Within each storytelling roundtable, narratives ranged from how Inuit boys bond with their fathers to how Inuit girls speak out about changing female roles in the community. Stories promoted humor, gave rise to debates about what was then and what should be now, and at times simply informed us about the Arctic way of life in the past and Inuit dreams for their future. Stories are especially relevant among aboriginal peoples, because stories sometimes rely more on oral transmission than on written accounts.

Roundtable learning presents an ideal forum for encouraging an entire community's active involvement. Because of its interactive approach, the circle provides a less hierarchical and less threatening structure for parents or extended families who have not felt welcome at school. Outsiders feel less threatened when learning includes their own probing questions and personal stories. Personal stories about one's cultural heritage can supplement textbook information in a cooperative roundtable setting.

Students from minority populations sometimes describe feeling put down when teachers deliver a one-sided view of any topic. These students cannot find their experiences in the content and resent the bias that usually accompanies a single perspective. Minority groups are not alone. As a student, I felt that my personal faith was often compromised. In high school and at university, I felt forced to express the atheistic views held by my instructors in order to do well in their classes. At roundtables, such subtle coercion is less likely to occur, since each participant brings her past knowledge and experience into the construction of new knowledge.

Students who resign themselves to passive roles represent the opposite of collaboration. Consider the words of *Their Way,* which was written and sung by Bob Blue in 1970 and sung to Anka's 1969 popular hit tune, *My Way:*

> I came, bought all my books, lived in the dorms, followed directions.
> I worked, I studied hard, met lots of folks who had connections.
> I crammed. They gave me grades, and may I say, not in a fair way.
> But more, much more than this, I did it their way.
>
> I learned all sorts of things, although I know I'll never use them.
> The courses that I took were all required. I didn't choose them.
> You'll find that to survive, it's best to act the doctrinaire way,
> And so I buckled down and did it their way.
>
> Yes, there were times I wondered why I had to crawl when I could fly.
> I had my doubts, but after all, I clipped my wings, and learned to crawl.
> I learned to bend, and in the end, I did it their way.
>
> And so, my fine young friends, now that I am a full professor,
> Where once I was oppressed, I've now become the cruel oppressor.
> With me, you'll learn to cope. You'll learn to climb life's golden stairway.
> Like me, you'll see the light, and do it their way.
>
> For what can I do? What can I do? Take out your books. Read Chapter Two.
> And if to you it seems routine, don't speak to me: Go see the dean.
> As long as they give me my pay, I'll do it their way.
>
> (Used with permission)

Through several intelligences, Bob considered the problem and wrote about the limitations that exist for many secondary and college students. This song provides a great launch for students' ideas on building roundtables. Had Bob Blue been a painter, he might have painted this response; or he could have created a debate or choreographed a dance to reflect the problem. Since the best solutions often come from give-and-take communications among people, collaboration paves the way for deeper ideas to emerge from areas that may otherwise be missed.

LISTENING ACTIVITIES TO ENSURE PARTICIPATION

Teachers are busy people who often lack the resources they need to make positive changes in their classrooms. Invariably, I am asked to suggest hands-on tools such as the listening activities included in this book.

According to students, few of their teachers listen well. This is unfortunate, because good listening can activate students' and teachers' skills and foster deeper understanding through a variety of perspectives. Faculty who hear from students are more apt to encourage their students to discover and develop unique abilities. When listened to, students are validated and affirmed. They tend to gain new confidence, which leads to more success at school.

GIFTS FROM ALL MEMBERS TO UNLEASH RESOLUTIONS

In many ways, the Inuit taught me the value of affirming every person's intellectual gifts and then creating an environment in which those gifts are nurtured and used. There are differences of opinion concerning how a range of opportunities should be created and about how knowledge should be tested and graded, but I have seen firsthand active learning modeled in enriched classrooms where a full range of intelligences is acknowledged and where students are happy and learning is personal. As illustrated in the following activities, teachers, students, and parents or invited guests can use circles in a variety of ways to enhance their work together. For each activity that follows, it is useful to start with outcomes that faculty or students expect. The activities that follow provide a step-by-step venue to achieve the outcome stated in your classes and faculty circles.

ACTIVITY 1.1   Meet Other Teachers

Outcome
To get to know other teachers well enough to begin working and learning together

Discussion and Procedure
Invite three or four teachers in your department or your area of the school to meet for lunch during the first month of the term. Ask questions about their personal and academic interests and abilities. Discuss ideas and materials each teacher requires for the term. Brainstorm ideas or materials that might be shared through a central banking system one of you can create. List topics each teacher will cover, so that other teachers may share resources that relate to the topics. Discuss evaluation techniques and methods. Are there evaluation tools that might be shared among classrooms? Is there any way that students from one classroom might be involved with students from another, such as for computer-based interviewing and writing projects? Set a regular time and place to meet with this group of teachers in order to network, share a meal, discuss concerns, and relate successful projects.

The idea is not to put more pressure on busy teachers, but to provide a helpful forum and network in order to build a community of learners among colleagues. Teachers I work with often express a desire for space and time to share with other faculty.

| ACTIVITY 1.2 | Creating a Newsletter to Build Bridges |

Outcome
A newsletter that includes notes from parents, students, and teachers, and that uses humor and cartoons as a common thread among the groups

Discussion and Procedure
Create a newsletter for parents and the school. Appoint as editors students who enjoy writing. Students who work with the paper might receive extra credit in writing or journalism.

The newsletter might contain letters of appreciation to or from parents after a school or class presentation. Letters should begin *Dear Mom and Dad, Dear Daughter,* or *Dear Son,* to protect students and parents from any embarrassment at school. Include humorous illustrations and text in each edition as a bridge among all groups. Students might use this paper as a forum for their best creative writing enterprises, for letters of concern, or as a way to share ideas with parents and teachers.

Encourage community or family members, students, and teachers to submit material. Invite the administration, counselors, and custodial staff to take part in the newsletter. Secondary students may invite parents to take an active role in gathering guest submissions and working with students on publication. Students or parents could sell the newsletter at secondary school functions to pay for art, photography, and paper.

| ACTIVITY 1.3 | Celebrate Your Gifts |

Outcome
A record of peer ideas of students' positive contributions in class

Discussion and Procedure
Inuit teachers on Baffin Island first taught me how to use the circle to solve difficult problems. In fact, I devised the notion of roundtable learning from this Inuit tradition, since it works well in any culture. It can also be used to give students an opportunity to celebrate each other's unique gifts.

The class sits in a circle for this activity. Each person receives a sheet of paper headed "The special gifts of . . ." After putting his or her name in the blank, each student passes the sheet to the person on the right, who lists one positive contribution that person makes to the class. Students continue passing papers to the right until each person has listed a contribution and the papers arrive back to their owners.

Encourage students to consider all the unique gifts mentioned and to take their peers' positive words seriously. Initially, you might display all papers with photos of owners on a Who's Who bulletin board. Eventually, encourage students to display their "gift sheets" in prominent places and to look at them whenever they feel discouraged or doubtful about their unique abilities. You should also participate in this circle and pass a sheet around for students' comments.

| ACTIVITY 1.4 | Mindscaping an Integrated Unit |

Outcome
A mindscape of a common theme, with four or five teachers organizing the integrated unit into four or five subtopics

Discussion and Procedure
In a roundtable approach to learning, every person comes to the circle as both learner and teacher to solve a group problem. A circle formation itself is not critical to this learning approach. The emphasis is on working together, creating a social environment where all students enjoy using their unique gifts to construct new knowledge. In roundtable learning, everyone works together to solve a problem or answer a key question. The question might be "How do we help teenagers use their unique gifts in school?" or "What should Canada do about hunger in nonindustrialized countries?" The group combines all their resources to solve each problem.

Mindscaping activities provide opportunities for teachers, students, and parents to learn together. Consider the following example of mindscaping for an integrated topic. With four or five other teachers, brainstorm for one common theme to teach. Use a mindscape to develop the main theme or question. Choose five subtopics, one for each teacher. Break down the subtopics into several lessons for each discipline represented. Make necessary connections among the disciplines. Choose outcomes and assessment strategies for each lesson. Illustrate the mindscape. Use color to show connections and suggest patterns. Discuss ways in which subtopics and lessons will relate to one another and ways in which they will not integrate. Ask for students' input before finalizing the mindscape. Display the mindscape as a poster on a central bulletin board for reference. Plan a shared project presentation night when you will display all final projects and discuss them with the participating classes and their parents. Record a brief summary of strategies that worked well and strategies that each teacher and class would change in future.

| ACTIVITY 1.5 | Observe Math Problem Solving |

Outcome
A clear understanding of a math concept through learning and teaching

Discussion and Procedure
When we create an opportune environment, students thrive in the role of teachers. But it is necessary to develop a safe environment from the beginning. This activity shows how students can enjoy and benefit from teaching problem-solving strategies to younger learners.

Students from one grade level pair with students from a lower grade level to teach a new math concept. Through observation and dialogue with the younger students, you will record the critical thinking skills of these younger children. In groups of three or four older and younger students, use the questions that follow to discuss the problem-solving skills you observe:

1. How did the older student first present the problem?
2. What helps or prompts did the older student provide?
3. What questions did the older student ask?
4. What questions did the younger student ask?
5. What did the younger student already know about this problem?
6. What new information did the younger student learn?
7. How did the younger student express mathematical thinking?
8. What can we learn about the younger student's thinking?
9. Did the younger student raise alternative methods or solutions?
10. What would the older student do differently next time?

Reflection on Personal Problem-Solving Skills
Use these questions to guide self-reflection:

1. What skills did the younger child demonstrate that were most like your own?
2. How were the younger child's thinking patterns different from yours?
3. How would you describe your own problem-solving approaches?

ACTIVITY 1.6 Dialogue Journal between Teachers and Students

Outcome
Shared thoughts and questions about classroom activities, ideas, beliefs, and learning approaches

Discussion and Procedure
All journal entries should be dated. Journals may include paragraphs, lists, and graphics. Students may use vertical lines to separate lists, such as pros listed on one side of the page and cons listed on the other. Students may use vertical lines or dialogue boxes for writer's comments on one side and other students' responses on the other side of the page. Students may use several approaches and topics, such as those that follow, for journal entries.

- expressing ideas about a curriculum topic
- brainstorming new approaches to solving a problem
- sequencing a response to a problem
- exploring pros and cons of a controversial issue
- raising questions about a discussion or reading
- communicating confusion about some aspect of the material being studied
- wondering about the feasibility of an experiment or hypothesis
- generating a progression of critical thinking exercises

Alternatives to this activity include *peer journaling,* in which students exchange journals with peers in order to interact about their learning, and *reflective individual journaling,* in which students write journals solely to explore and reflect on their own learning.

| ACTIVITY 1.7 | Creating a Dream Speech |

Outcome
Dream speeches

Discussion and Procedure
This activity will encourage students to express their unique worldviews and to shape their own personal dreams in your classroom.

Students consider specific ideas they care a great deal about and talk them over with friends. They list a few of their best ideas. In groups of three or four, they read together Dr. Martin Luther King Jr.'s "I Have a Dream" speech. They compare their dreams and ideas to King's and, using the same style, create an outline. First, students explore who King was and why he cared about the vision for freedom described in his speech. Then they explore an issue that affects them and their peers in a deep way and use similar approaches to describe their insights for change and improvement in that area.

After checking the outline with peer editors or you, students write their speeches. Speeches should relate specifically to them and should be similar to King's speech in form and length. Present speeches to classmates or to parents and community members at a special evening where parents and friends join you for an "I Have a Dream" evening.

A rubric for the evening might include the following criteria. The "I Have a Dream" presentation should

- Engage all or most of the intelligences.

- Demonstrate a current issue that most people in the audience would relate to.

- Show illustrations of your strengths or weaknesses in search of solutions.

- Illustrate possibilities beyond the problems.

- Contain results of research done to discover what others think and why.

- Make realistic predictions about why your dream will bring improvements.

- Compare King's ideals for freedom with the ideals expressed in your dream.

| ACTIVITY 1.8 | Ask a Probing Question |

Outcome
Probing curriculum questions developed with four other teachers in an effort to learn more about the issues

Discussion and Procedure
Each person writes down one personally probing two-footed question. One foot should relate to the interests and abilities of students you teach, and the other foot

should be shaped to get the results you expect from content. The question may concern change in your classroom, gender issues, curriculum topics, and so on. In groups of five teachers, each person gets a number from 1 to 5. Person 2 asks a question. Person 3 responds to the question. Person 4 adds one aspect not found in Person 3's answer, without repeating any part of that answer. Person 5 adds a final response to the question, without repeating anything already said. Person 1 repeats the question and summarizes the responses. Repeat the process, with members taking turns asking questions, responding, and summing up.

After questions are shared and discussed, develop a simple plan for using more two-footed questions to raise motivation and achievement in your classes. Test your questions with students and discuss why some questions get more engaged responses. Then adjust your questions that raised less discussion in order to engage more students. What made the difference in questions that generated roundtable think tanks on a topic and those that met with little response from students?

ACTIVITY 1.9   Parents' Interest Inventory

Outcome
A completed inventory by each parent of students' skills

Discussion and Procedure
Questions are vehicles to bring parents into the classroom community. Ask parents about their teens and help them help you with an interest inventory, such as the one that follows. (The inventory was adapted from Campbell, Campbell, and Dickinson, 1992, p. 143.) Parents can complete the inventory at the beginning of each term and return it to you to include in students' portfolios.

- Three words that describe my teen are . . .
- Things my teen does when not in school are . . .
- My teen would benefit from learning more about . . .
- Someday my teen would like to . . .
- Learning is fun for my teen when . . .
- If my teen could have anything at school, it would be . . .
- My teen likes to get praise for . . .
- At school, when my teen does something well, she likes to be acknowledged by . . .
- My teen wonders a lot about . . .
- My teen likes people who . . .
- Sometimes my teen worries about . . .
- One thing that really bothers my teen is . . .
- Something that really challenges my teen is . . .
- One thing I know about my teen is . . .

ACTIVITY 1.10   What You Know and Want to Know

Outcome
Students' understanding of what they know about a topic and what they would like to find out

Discussion and Procedure
Questions can open a door into a student's interests and abilities. This activity probes what students know and want to know about the curriculum topic. Students relate the new topic to their own experiences by describing what facts or insights they already know about any aspect of it and then listing a few questions they have about the topic. In groups of three or four, students decide what they would most like to find out about this topic. They consider some activities or projects that would allow them to explore the topic further.

DEVELOPING CURRICULUM THROUGH QUESTIONS

Questions can also enable groups to create meaningful curricula. In a roundtable social studies teacher training course in Pangnirtung and Igloolik, preservice teachers investigated strategies to teach the Northwest Territories social studies curricula. Together, we designed activities that would generate critical thinking, problem solving, and decision making among Inuit students. Our questions may be similar to those you have asked. Or they may foster discussions among colleagues and students that will lead to a collaboration of ideas for your upcoming unit.

Questions lead to new discoveries because you look at life through new lenses. You become more like a private detective about why a few teens have poor attitudes than a judge deciding whose fault it might be. If you take your problem to the Internet, you might find that some problems are connected to how the human brain functions. For example, you might not have known that you can correct a poor attitude with hydration. The following Website offers a place where parents and teachers share ideas about heat dehydration: http://www.defeattheheat.com/dehydration_and_kids.html. This site states, "Early signs of dehydration may include: thirst, irritability, headache, dizziness, muscle cramping, nausea, vomiting, weakness, decreased performance, heat sensations, general discomfort."

Inuit teachers-in-training and I developed our course, "How People Learn Best," mainly through a roundtable method of questioning. Our concern was the same as every teacher's: *How can we make learning relevant, meaningful, and enjoyable?* Through questions, we explored the following topics:

1. How can cultural diversity assist learning?
2. How can we engage the disengaged student?
3. How can we spark a cooperative spirit in classrooms?
4. How can we boost students' thinking skills?
5. How can teachers promote independent student learners?
6. How can we access both sides of the brain?

7. How can students create child-centered classrooms?

8. How can we welcome parents into the learning process?

9. How do students discover their personal learning profiles?

10. How can we use the vast resources around us?

11. How does one develop critical and creative thinking?

12. How can we improve memory skills?

Through these key questions, we focused on specific curriculum goals. These questions also helped us shape clear learning outcomes and provided an accurate assessment tool to evaluate these outcomes. Outcomes include knowledge, skills, attitudes, values, and social responsibilities. In each case we were concerned with three questions.

1. What do students already know about this topic?

2. What is the desired outcome?

3. What stages must a student pass through to go from current knowledge to the desired outcome?

Once we resolved these questions, we generated the following activities to help students move from current knowledge toward the following desired outcomes:

1. Identify how culture can enhance learning.

2. Adapt the curriculum to engage the disengaged students.

3. Increase the cooperative spirit in the classroom.

4. Improve the teachers' own thinking skills.

5. Negotiate assessment with students.

6. Access both sides of the brain in the learning process.

7. Create child-centered classrooms.

8. Include parents in the learning process.

9. Identify teachers' own learning profiles.

10. Use increased number of and higher-quality resources.

11. Develop students' critical and creative thinking.

12. Use strategies to help students improve memory skills.

Clearly listed course expectations provide students of any age with ideas about where to begin. We welcomed community members into all roundtable discussions. Inuit parents and elders sat in our circles as learning partners. We deliberated about curriculum outcomes and activities. Not surprisingly, the community came up with rich ideas, such as traveling on the tundra overnight with an elder. We chose activities to guide us toward common outcomes.

How does one introduce meaningful questions in roundtable learning? To assess your own skills, you might begin with a central question and brainstorm for solutions. Assign a recorder to list all responses on chart paper. You will devise rules appropriate for your class and questions that challenge.

After the roundtable discussion, reflect on the process. First ask, "Did I create a sense of wonder and curiosity before the lesson started?" Then use the following questions to determine whether you created opportunities for each person to participate:

1. How often did I talk?

2. How often did students talk?

3. Who talked most? Why?

4. Are there other activities or questions that would have helped students discover more new knowledge?

5. Did I tell students or ask them?

6. How did I motivate students for this particular lesson? Did my motivation strategy work? Why? Why not?

7. Did students ask questions?

In a later section, we will consider more detailed questioning and discuss what kinds of questions work best. We will consider how good questions can lead learners to various levels of thinking and suggest examples of how good questions prime the critical faculties, while improperly constructed questions can ruin creative thinking. For instance, questions that lack any specific connection to students will discourage many from looking for an answer. In addition, questions that interest students but fail to probe the content will encourage superficial thinking.

To value good questions as a guide to learning is to value good listening skills. Successful roundtable learning relies heavily on successful listening practices, such as those that follow:

1. Brainstorm with students to discover what the term *active listening* really means. Write their suggestions on the board or chart paper and leave them up. Students may list the following characteristics: a nod of recognition, eye contact, probing questions to the speaker, and the ability to recall and discuss main statements.

2. Conduct a talking circle. Students take turns holding a small object of some significance. Nobody but the one holding the object may speak. That person presents her perspectives, opinions, and ideas about the issue being discussed. When she has finished making her statement, she passes the object to the next person. Everyone has an opportunity to speak. Quiet students love this activity!

3. Have students interview one another on the lesson topic. The interviewer then reports orally what the other person said. Give the interviewee an opportunity to change or explain anything in the oral report.

4. Tell the class that there will be a brief quiz at the end of the day. The quiz will cover only the ideas shared by the students during the day. In other words, students will quote one another's ideas and then defend or oppose them, based on their own understanding of what was stated and what supports they have for or against. This task works well only in a roundtable that employs a careful "tone" so that all students hear and are heard. When tone is taught so that students value one another, they learn to disagree and add to answers without diminishing any other person. So the results produce win-win responses to complex issues. It might be a good idea to teach tone in stages, starting with the reminder to say

three positive things about another's ideas and then show specific reasons and supports for agreeing or disagreeing.

5. During group discussions, remind the class what good listening skills are. Avoid singling out any one student.

6. Divide the class into two concentric circles, placing all of the girls in one circle and the boys in the other. The inner circle pretends the opposite sex is absent and talks about an issue from their gender's point of view. The outer circle is there in ears only! For example, you might start with an inner circle of boys, who will discuss the topic from a male perspective and tell what is different from the girls' perspective. Girls will listen intently without speaking or gesturing. Then have students change places so that girls are inside and boys listen. Many wonderful ideas and issues emerge through this activity. Teams are always surprised to find out what the other sex really thinks!

At this point you may wish to illustrate to students how male and female brains differ biologically. Then help them work out a plan to work together so that more is gained from both genders.

Researchers suggest, and teachers affirm, that males tend to use more math proficiency, spatial ability, and aggression, whereas females tend to include more language, emotion, and nurture. Both aspects are needed: some boys are more nurturing than girls, and some girls surpass boys on math scores. Biological brain differences help explain gender differences, and this knowledge can help faculty promote more strengths from both genders.

The corpus callosum, which connects the two hemispheres of the brain, concentrates the connection on one side in males and the other in females. The connections tend to crisscross to both sides of females' brains, which helps them integrate ideas and see relationships, while a male's corpus callosum connects in a way that encourages a focus on one task at a time.

When classroom communities help students develop their individual mental strengths, students will learn to overcome feelings of intimidation and to avoid putting themselves down or acting superior.

For more than 30 years, I have interviewed faculty and students across genders, cultures, and careers in order to understand how women and men use their brains differently, with the goal of improving respect for both genders. Everywhere I found ways to encourage basic differences, so that people can enjoy more respect and value others' perspectives.

7. Discuss openly with students what it feels like to be ignored when you speak. Have students share their own experiences of being ignored or criticized for sharing an idea. Encourage them to express how that experience affected their willingness to share additional ideas and listen attentively to their personal stories. Discuss problems of listening and ask if they have recognized similar problems in themselves and others. They might reflect in journals about their own listening strengths and weaknesses. Suggest and share strategies for improving personal listening.

8. Discuss listening problems that students recognize as occurring across cultures or between the sexes. Ask what they have observed about how teachers and students listen or how they listen to their peers. What are the problems? What are possible solutions?

9. Read an interesting or funny story and then test students about one or two of the big ideas. With this activity, students can enjoy and also reap the benefits of listening. This activity promotes an awareness to stop and really listen.

Questions That Identify
Individual Abilities

To help students clarify what their intellectual gifts are, ask them the following questions:

1.   What three words best describe you?

2.   In one brief sentence, describe what you like to do most.

3.   About what subject do you most enjoy learning?

4.   What activities do you persist in improving?

5.   If you could expand our thinking in one area, what would you tell us?

6.   What hobbies do you enjoy and do well in?

7.   What do others say about your talents?

8.   List three topics that you know a lot about.

9.   Describe one skill that you have developed. Tell how you have perfected the skill through practice.

10.   What TV programs do you enjoy, and why?

11.   What books have you read during the last year, and what did you like most about them?

12.   Describe your ideal learning environment.

Journal writing helps students identify and reflect on their individual interests and abilities. Journals, especially written online, can also help identify students' learning preferences. My Inuit student teachers' writing, for instance, confirmed spatial and bodily-kinesthetic gifts and showed a preference to write on the computer. Knowing this, I was able to help them to develop a social studies curriculum that would use their strengths and help them develop their skills in English, their second language. We worked online and also built mock communities, which were used as a visual background to their oral stories about community traditions and plans for the future.

IMPLICATIONS OF QUESTIONING
IN ROUNDTABLE LEARNING CIRCLES

In this chapter you have read about roundtable approaches to learning in which students explore any topic through probing questions. The following list of activities came from exploring one such roundtable question—"What activities would create a unit for appreciating the Arctic climate?" In this activity, students' talents acted as learning tools in the following ways:

- Photography would show the variations of climate throughout each season.

- Music would illustrate a river of glacial ice making its way to the ocean.

- Drama groups would create tableaux for family activities in each season.

- Computer programs would promote interactive discussions and science stations.

- Speeches would be good vehicles for communicating the history of the Ice Age.

- Art would illustrate haiku or essays about a favorite season.

- Innovative group projects would describe climactic changes.

- Students could develop and play games or create dances about earth's tilt, which places the North Pole in darkness for nearly six months of the year.

- Biographical essays would describe how Inuit families or animals have adapted to the cold.

- Choral groups would create poetry recitals describing aspects of snow, ice, and the tundra.

- Study guide creation would enable the review of historic and scientific texts.

- Lists or visual time lines would show the year's sequence of climactic events from winter to summer solstice.

- Interviews or impersonations would introduce real people or fictitious characters who survived Arctic storms.

- Students could reenact early Inuit lives or create a newspaper that described their adaptations to fierce climactic conditions.

Inuit teachers often modeled how working together helps everyone realize their abilities. When I first arrived in the Arctic, I asked myself what I could possibly teach these Inuit people, who have survived for generations in this remote, wonderful, terrible land. In fact, it bothered me that so many non-Inuit peoples positioned themselves as educational leaders in the Arctic. For this reason, Inuit culture seemed to have less influence in some schools than northern people wanted. In response to my own question, I scribbled in the margin of my psychology text: *The Arctic is really our teacher; I am a novice student among these people.* In roundtable, we frequently reverse roles. Interestingly, in the last few years the Inuit have taken over educational leadership and restored their own culture to the curriculum.

Through probing questions, Inuit students helped me share in their ways while I worked among them. On many occasions, it seemed to me that we worked together to bind cultures and harmonize beliefs in order to write a curriculum that they would teach. Over time, they became more my colleagues than adult students I taught. Our combined laughter warmed harsh blizzard lands and brought sunlight to long dark days. I like to think that, just as music mixes words with tunes, we joined together to create one song.

LEARNING FROM VARIOUS CULTURES

Perhaps more than any other time in history, we face possibilities of questioning and learning with others who share very diverse cultural emphases. Through such collaboration, we begin to recognize and enjoy the wide variety of people and their ideas. But how many times has the circle been silenced by one voice? To learn together requires a new formation in our classrooms, one that will allow for equal participation in the learning process. In Inuktitut, one would say *sanaqatigiinig,* which means "working together."

Now that you have identified the core components of effective circles, you are ready to build curriculum for a class you will teach. Students I interviewed over several years, from Canada, to England, to South America to Mexico to Baffin Island, have helped to identify several critical curriculum requirements for successful roundtable curriculum projects.

For example, students expressed the fact that peers contribute significantly to their learning. Learners recommended that faculty encourage more community involvement, especially in the development of curriculum content. Interestingly, students confirmed several recommendations that are currently supported in the research literature on educational change. I refer to the recommendations for renewal from Sizer's (1992) Coalition of Essential Schools and his proposed scenario for Horace's School of the Future (pp. 60 and 89). I also reference Sarason's (1991) recommendations regarding integration (p. 163), where he describes an overarching goal for students. You will find other similarities in Fullan's (1996) collaborative case studies (pp. 49, 50, 79, 80, 93, and 95), where faculty move from research into best practices and back.

Chapter 2 takes this research and the roundtable learning activities in this chapter another step, as secondary or college students build interactive centers in order to share and engage others in their project ideas.

Learning Communities Take Many Shapes

It is pleasing to think that somewhere in our minds perhaps lies a building waiting to be built, a grand unified theory of physics, the beautiful song of a hermit thrush, a sentence waiting to be written.

Alan Lightman (Canadian author and mathematician)

A new Multiple Intelligence Community Education and Family Center has been established in Rockford, Illinois. The center is an autonomous, nonprofit, community-based organization. Rockford's community center reminds us that learning communities take many shapes. Details on the Internet (http://new horizons.org/home.html) describe the multimodal services offered:

Vocational assessment, counseling, and job-seeking services (including job-retention support)

Vocational education in areas such as office technology, retail and financial services, child-care certification, housekeeping, medical transcription, and machine technology

Personalized tutoring in math and English

Counseling and social-service support for the non-English-speaking refugees (translation, medical and legal services, immigration and naturalization)

Recycling depositories for used household and business goods

Subcontract support for manufacturing businesses in the area (assembly, packaging, quality inspection) and information processing (medical and legal documents)

You can't help but notice all the connections that link learning to life beyond traditional classrooms. This special learning community combines a multiple intelligence approach with a productive work environment. The community operates on the belief that work is a common unifying value in society, a cornerstone of successful social relationships. In fact, the community provides full- or part-time employment for more than two hundred persons, making it one of Rockford's 100 largest employers.

The community's contact person, Judy Bonne, has written extensively about the site. Judy describes other schools that have broken away from the passive lecture hall model in favor of a vibrant living community that creates a sense of invitation, openness, and wonder.

But what about those of us still teaching in egg-crate schools, where subjects stand as isolated entities and where there is little interaction among teachers? Even in those schools where students attend traditional classroom lessons, roundtable communities are possible. Most of this chapter outlines a roundtable approach for teaching a unit that integrates a variety of subjects and yet is taught in one class with one teacher. The ideal approach would probably be to collaborate with several teachers first and then to apply an integrated mix of best practices that teachers find useful.

This chapter focuses on one specific topic, "Life and culture in Brazil," in order to illustrate how a roundtable approach to integration and community building can enhance even the most traditional schools. Each sample lesson offered here is intended to act as a guide or idea bank for different topics that you may teach over any one-month period. Whether you teach lessons that relate to Brazil or to another topic, you'll want to discuss strategies with colleagues. Idea sharing often starts by communicating with another interested teacher or parent in your school. Once you connect with another innovative person, others are more likely to join the circle as you progress and develop ideas for your classes.

CREATING ROUNDTABLES AT STAFF MEETINGS

Staff rooms provide ideal starting places to create roundtables, where faculty can generate questions and form solutions about curriculum changes. The best roundtables take place at interactive staff meetings that involve curriculum-centered discussions.

What images come to mind when you think of faculty meetings you attend? Do you envision think tanks for creative contributions around compelling issues? Roundtable interactions at faculty meetings will transform staff rooms from battlefields or complaint arenas into places where insights or professional ideas germinate. When staff rooms are organized to discuss and share best practices, faculty come with this expectancy. When faculty share best practices, they find solutions for problems they face in their classes, and their students prosper. In fact, a faculty room climate will indicate a great deal about any school's success.

Tom Burns, a shop teacher at one large urban school in which I consulted, regularly turned off both his hearing aids as soon as staff meetings began. Tom would then sleep with his eyes open, while the others read boring reports and made housekeeping announcements for an hour each week. Tom's habit of tuning out lasted for a dozen years until he finally retired. But on the very few occasions when faculty discussed curriculum or interacted about a challenging educational article they had read, Tom joined in enthusiastically. Tom was creative, gifted, and an inspiring teacher whom students loved. At his retirement party, parents came in droves to express their appreciation for Tom's teaching skills and care for students. But at faculty meetings, Tom felt bored and disinterested. Many faculty describe faculty meetings as a waste of time. How many faculty meetings share meaningful educative issues such as good learning and teaching methods? But in the best learning communities faculty meetings provide a roundtable opportunity to celebrate the diverse gifts within a teaching community. These gatherings are not run by one man or woman nor are they chiefly reporting sessions. Instead, they facilitate vibrant exchanges in which people are valued and where key ideas discussed run deeper than any one or two interpretations or opinions. Roundtables are tools that can help change the culture from negative or stagnant into positive and interactive.

Genuine renewal, however, will inevitably necessitate changes in deeply rooted status quo issues, such as top-down faculty meetings or power and control behaviors. Curricular success is more likely when faculty allow the seeds of reform to root under the nutrients of many participants. Successful faculty often report that changes are not as dependent on acquiring more money as they are on creating new structures based on inspiring ideas and practical plans.

As you create and develop MITA units that suit your content and student needs, you and your students will identify which parts of the lesson worked well and which did not. This will help create classroom communities where more students will report positive results. The best thought sprouts feet and wings. Some faculty put lesson banks online in order to share new materials and ideas with colleagues.

The MITA materials and lesson ideas provided in the next section can lead to the positive results that come whenever students and faculty think and create innovative solutions together. This case example involves smaller roundtables, which students then build into centers where they explore facts and demonstrate their understanding from multiple perspectives.

A ROUNDTABLE APPROACH TO STUDYING BRAZIL

You might use the following eight-center design for any high school or college interdisciplinary topic. This curriculum used Brazil as the topic. In our study of Brazil, the community came together to interact with students and to enjoy Brazilian cuisine prepared by this class. The final projects integrated math, English, social studies, and science. Our work was concentrated in the mornings so that students could participate in their electives and other disciplines in the afternoons.

Our experience drew support and encouragement from the entire community, who were involved from the beginning. Parents were invited to a meeting in September to share their ideas and offer suggestions for the project. They supplied resources and gave support during the month. They often interacted with their teenagers.

At the end of the project, we displayed the entire finished work for the community. For two days, our gym could have been mistaken for a pocket of Brazil or a Brazilian museum. Lively music played in the background and specially prepared food filled a banquet table. Posters, collages, colorful graphs, maps, and typed essays covered the gym's cement walls. On tables lay topographic representations, dioramas, models, scientific discoveries, architectural mock-ups, and student portfolios. Students interacted in lively discussions and demonstrated Brazilian lifestyles, art, history, industry, sports, and culture at the eight topic centers.

Parents were thrilled to see their teens in the roles of experts, and teens enjoyed sharing their hard work and unique projects. Community members responded to students' oral presentations and encouraged heated debates. Through one group's slide shows and the ensuing discussions, we learned of Brazil's distinctive qualities as well as of our group's abilities and talents to communicate. We better understood differences among cultures within our community and grew to appreciate each person's unique qualities.

Questions from Students

To make this topic relevant and meaningful, our lessons began with students' questions. We introduced the unit by laying out the bare bones of the curriculum and briefly describing ways in which we might create the eight centers. Students offered suggestions, ideas, and concerns. They asked the following questions:

1. Who chooses our groups? Can we have a say in where we work?
2. Will reference books be available in the classroom?
3. How much computer time will we have?
4. Who will pay for materials?
5. What happens if one group member is expected to do most of the work?
6. Will other tests and major assignments be postponed during the work?
7. Will there be class time to work together?
8. How will we be tested on our work?
9. Who keeps our group projects?

Students' questions and concerns guided our discussions from the start of the project. As a group, we responded to each question to the satisfaction of each participant. From these efforts, we developed an activity that helped promote a safe environment for students' questioning.

Guidelines for Student-Generated Questions

The following list may help you and your students in discussing for deeper understanding each of these categories of questions:

- **Questions to identify past experiences.** For example, *How does what happens here compare to what happened in your experience?*

- **Table of contents questions.** For example, *What might you find most interesting about this book, based on its table of contents?*

- **Headline questions.** For example, *In today's news headlines, what major story affects your life most, and why is that so?*

- **Vocabulary questions.** For example, *What action words are used to describe the most significant event in this story, and what do they tell you about that event?*

- **Questions that encourage deeper understanding.** For example, *Why do you suppose the character you read about acted the way she did, and what might have resulted if she had acted in another way?*

- **Questions about main ideas.** For example, *How would you describe the main idea if you were asked to create a bumper sticker to highlight today's lesson?*

- **Questions for sorting out details.** For example, *What were the main events that led up to . . . , and, in your opinion, what significance do these events add?*

- **Questions about sequence.** For example, *If you had been in charge, how might you have changed the order of events here, and why?*

- **Questions about inference.** For example, *Can you identify three things that are inferred here and show how each could affect a teenager's ability to do well at school?*

- **Questions of personal relevance.** For example, *How did what happened change your ideas about . . . ?* (Weber, 1999, pp. 188–189)

Prompts for Student-Generated Questions

Since student-generated questions are new to some students, it is useful to supply tasks and prompts that can help students enjoy and benefit from generating their own questions. Your guidance can help them come up with some terrific results.

Questions to identify past experiences

- What do you already know about . . . ?

- How do you know that . . . ?

- What do you think of when . . . ?

Table of contents questions

- What ideas about . . . do you get from the table of contents?

- What significant facts do you expect to find in . . . ?

- Why is this different than (or is similar to) . . . ?

Headline questions

- Main ideas are indicated by . . . ?

- Questions that arise from these headlines are . . . ?

- Organization of these headlines suggests . . . ?

Vocabulary questions

- Three words you may not know are . . . ?

- The glossary tells us significant information about . . . ?

- What words may others not know that you do know the meaning of?

Questions that encourage deeper understanding

- Can you describe why . . . ?

- Do you find evidence to support . . . ?

- What is main problem here, and how is it solved?

Questions about main ideas

- What is the main idea of the chapter?

- What would be a good heading for each main paragraph?

- What are the chief points the author makes?

Questions for sorting out details

- What facts prove that . . . ?

- When did you know the author's intention?
- What evidence supports the main claim?

Questions about sequence

- What are the ten most important steps to follow in . . . ?
- What four preliminary steps would help . . . ?
- How is sequence important here?

Questions about inference

- What significance does this have for you?
- What type of a person was . . . ?
- What do you think will be the consequences of . . . ?

Questions of personal relevance

- What did the author say that you will apply personally?
- How would you react to . . . ?
- What section of the chapter elicits feelings of appreciation? (Weber, 1999, pp. 188–189)

Designing the Unit Using Brain-Friendly Tactics

Following is a discussion of Howard Gardner's eight ways of learning (see Weber, 1999, p. 14) that are used in this book's brain-compatible approach. Students were encouraged to use multiple approaches to explore the ideas and then to present their ideas through different intelligences. To ensure that students learned the material and met high standards for their presentations, they were expected to create a rubric for each presentation. Each rubric would have five criteria that showed expectations for the projects. Faculty added several criteria to those of the students as deemed necessary to ensure deep understanding of the topics.

Research sources for this unit included the library, museums, Website investigations, surveys, dialogues, experts' insights, e-mail exchanges with a Brazilian secondary school, textbooks, lived experience, relevant research articles, and media coverage.

In the centers they constructed, students incorporated Brazil's multifaceted history and lifestyles. The bodily-kinesthetic center included dance and sports; the math center, economy, population, and inventions; the verbal-linguistic center, education and language; the music center, music and culture; the spatial center, art and architecture; the interpersonal center, lifestyle and relationships; the intrapersonal center, a day in the life of a Brazilian; and the naturalistic center, a description of where the condor is seen and its description as a key symbol of Brazilian life and hope.

In each instance, students were asked to state which class of Brazilians they were researching or describing—the lower, middle, or upper class. For each center, students began by creating a title for the center and then submitted guiding questions for the center (the key questions to which they will respond). Students then

listed the resources and materials they required and indicated where they expected to find them briefly described the steps for completing the work, suggesting reasonable deadlines for each stage

outlined, in collaboration with other students, their criteria for evaluation

stated what specific qualities they expected to evaluate with you to ensure they understood the materials researched

Bodily-Kinesthetic Center

Key questions for this center were:

1. Who are three well-known dancers in Brazil who would appeal to your friends?

2. For what are these three known in addition to dance?

3. Learn and perform one or more of their dances.

4. How does Brazilian dance compare to other dances you know about?

5. Where are the famous carnivals in Brazil? What challenges people to support these?

6. Reproduce a dance carnival that might be performed in Brazil.

7. Who are two well-known athletes in Brazil?

8. Can you represent their sports using several of Gardner's eight ways of knowing?

9. Why has soccer become famous in Brazil? Describe the game as they play it. Demonstrate a game.

10. Can you describe the art of sailing in Brazil as it is done for fun and competition?

11. Describe or represent the sport you most enjoy as it would be played in Brazil.

12. How can you integrate the ideas you come up with to present one coherent center that will teach others about the details of dance and sports in Brazil?

Mathematical-Logical Center

Key questions for this center were:

1. What are the most popular math-related careers in Brazil? What training do they require?

2. For what purposes are computers used? Who owns them?

3. In what ways, if any, do Brazilian schools use computers?

4. What is the average salary for teens in Brazil? Graph some comparative wages.

5. Using recent statistics, show where Brazilian wealth is concentrated and why.

6. Using graphs or posters, indicate the industries that have helped Brazil most.

7. Where are the greatest concentrations of people in Brazil?

8. How has the demography influenced prosperity and poverty in Brazilian communities?

9. Represent some of the most innovative scientific Brazilian inventions.

10. Who created these inventions? How?

11. Using only numbers, create a poster showing how you would describe Brazil.

12. What would a grade 10 math class in Brazil look like? A grade 10 science class?

Verbal-Linguistic Center

Key questions for this center were:

1. In 500 or fewer words, relate the history of Brazil.

2. In what ways have events in Brazilian history influenced other parts of the world, in your opinion?

3. Describe any progress in education and literacy over the past ten years.

4. What would a day in the life of a Brazilian grade 10 class be like? Represent a day in a Brazilian school through role-play, poetry, or debate.

5. In what ways has Brazilian education influenced other parts of the world?

6. What types of people receive education in Brazil? Write a one-act play about the most educated people.

7. What people tend to be illiterate in Brazil? Stage a mock interview to show why this is so, report your results, and suggest solutions to the literacy problem.

8. Describe the news media in Brazil. What TV, radio, magazines, and films are popular?

9. Create a newspaper that illustrates one day in the life of a Brazilian.

10. Using photography or photographs from magazines, create a scrapbook; add one or more stories for each illustration.

11. Interview a grade 10 Brazilian teacher through the Internet. Ask the teacher to describe Brazilian educational concerns and highlights. Include the interview in a report.

12. Discuss the community's involvement in education and compare or contrast parental involvement in your own community.

Musical-Rhythmic Center

Key questions for this center were:

1. Write a song in the style of some of the most popular music teens enjoy in Brazil.

2. What Brazilian classical musicians are well known among their teens?

3. What Brazilian folk and country musicians are well known?

4. What Brazilian jazz and popular musicians are well known?

5. How is music taught in Brazilian high schools?

6. Identify Brazilian music in a film and show its influence on the story.

7. What would a typical middle-class family in Brazil eat in one day?

8. Write a poem or song about foods popular for working-class Brazilians?

9. Create music to describes a menu for a typical poor family in Brazil?

10. Where is Brazilian coffee grown, and to what countries is it exported? Describe this process through music.

11. Write a song that describes a typical day in Brazil for a grade 10 student.

12. Use music to describe an important aspect of Brazilian life, from your perspective.

Visual-Spatial Center

Key questions for this center were:

1. Who are Brazil's best-known artists, from your perspective?

2. How has Brazilian art influenced art in other parts of the world?

3. What Brazilian events honor artists and celebrate art?

4. How does a typical Brazilian artist's life differ from that of an artist in your community?

5. How is art taught in grade 10?

6. Where are Brazil's art institutions? What do they offer artists?

7. What types of art would be displayed in a large Brazilian art gallery?

8. Describe two well-known architects in Brazil.

9. In what ways do the works of these two architects differ? How are they similar?

10. Represent some of the architectural designs popular in Brazil.

11. Design three typical Brazilian homes—one for the poor, one for the middle class, one for the wealthy. Using a mock-up, indicate the vulnerability of homes to natural elements.

12. Using any art form, describe one day in the life of a Brazilian teen from a middle-class family.

Interpersonal Center

Key questions for this center were:

1. Using Gardner's eight ways of knowing, represent a Brazilian family and describe its class privileges or disadvantages.

2. Role-playing several key Brazilian historical people, put on a radio talk show and discuss how family life relates to politics.

3. Describe Brazil's story through the lives of each member of one imaginary Brazilian family.

4. What are the major religions in Brazil? Who leads them and why?

5. Who decides how communities will live and interact and with what results?

6. How have Brazilians influenced and been influenced by other parts of the world?

7. What do Brazilians wear? What do they care about? What do they want for their future?

8. Using the Internet, ask a Brazilian leader to describe leadership in Brazil.

9. How do Brazilians relate to teenagers?

10. How do Brazilian men relate to women? Brazilian women to men?

11. To what countries do Brazilian exports go? Who exports to Brazil?

12. In what ways have Brazilian people changed over the past ten years?

Intrapersonal Center

Key questions for this center were:

1. Write your personal reflections on one Brazilian leader's life.

2. What would you experience if you were to spend two weeks in a Brazilian teen's home?

3. What would you do for a living if you lived in Brazil? Describe your day using any of Gardner's eight ways of knowing.

4. What would you eat if you lived in a Brazilian community?

5. What would you like to say to Brazil's current leaders?

6. If you were a dog, how would you spend one day in any Brazilian community?

7. What important beliefs would you hold if you had grown up in Brazil?

8. As a sailor living in Brazil, what would your weekend entail?

9. Pretend you are a well-known Brazilian philosopher being interviewed on TV. Film or photograph and tape-record your interview. Write out the interview using a typewriter or word processor.

10. What would you like to say to Brazilian teens about life, education, values, art, and music?

11. Create a diary that illustrates one week in a Brazilian grade 10 class. You may use art or any of Gardner's other ways of expressing your thoughts.

12. If you could help one very poor Brazilian community by improving lifestyles in a realistic way, what would you do?

Naturalistic Center

Key questions for this center were:

1. From the perspective of a condor, tell why Brazilian people would benefit from your position as a sacred symbol that represents power, strength, and success of native Brazilians.

2. Describe a day in the life of a Brazilian condor.

3. Illustrate the problems in Brazil that threaten the condor's existence.

4. What would the condor advise or hear from people of Brazil concerning native rights?

5. List the most distinctive habits of the Brazilian condor.

6. What do condors and spiritual beliefs share in common?

7. How would the condor improve Brazilian lifestyles so that humans and nature could both benefit and prosper?

8. How is the condor a symbol of courage?

9. Relate one myth or play in which the condor plays a central role.

10. In your opinion, why is the condor considered by many to be a sacred bird?

11. How is the condor a symbol of death and rebirth in South America?

12. Illustrate the condor as a sign or symbol of native rights.

Students used the following Website in thinking about how people, beliefs, and life in Brazil compare to a condor's life: http://www.spub.ksu.edu/issues/v100/sp/n130/cam-harald-prins-shell.html.

Using the Internet to Gather and Exchange Ideas

A great resource of information about Brazil or any country can be found on the Internet. To start, you may wish to begin with a Yahoo, Google, or Dogpile search engine for information. The URL for Brazil is http://www.yahoo.com/Regional/countries/Brazil/. To search for information on any other country, simply exchange the word *Brazil* in the address for whatever country you are looking for. You can find lesson creation ideas at: http://www.sites4teachers.com/links/redirect .php?url=http://www.adprima.com/lesson.htm.

From the Internet search, you'll find specific information on your topic. Let's say you are researching Joao Batista Villanova Artigas, one of the more important Brazilian architects. You will find photos of the architecture created by this remarkable modern Brazilian architect at http://www.lsi.usp.br/~artigas/home/. His works displayed on the Internet include the University of Sao Paulo School of Architecture, the Morumbi Stadium, Jau Bus Terminal, Lavara Industry, Santapaula Marina, and Itanhaem Gimnasium.

Using information and photos from the Internet, you can reproduce posters displaying Artigas's work, or you can write about the work and compare it to architecture from other areas. You may want to show how Artigas's work compares to that of his peers, how it has changed from early architecture, and how you would add to or subtract from the work. Be careful of copyright requirements, which are usually listed at each Internet site. Often the author requests you explain how you intend to use the material. It is important that all Internet users practice this courtesy.

The goal is to empower students to find accurate facts and then to use their multiple intelligences to apply these facts to real-life situations. This is the key characteristic of roundtable or fireside circles. The active engagement with facts in solving real-life problems leads to deeper understanding and relevance for more students. The best roundtable or brain-based teaching creates spaces for this to happen, regardless of the topic taught.

Assessment Strategies for the Brazil Unit

In addition to the individual groups' assessment criteria, we developed a set of standards common to all centers. Each project, we concluded, should meet the following criteria:

- provide rich contexts as backgrounds to the study
- relate to real-life situations in Brazil
- display knowledge, skills, and understanding about the topic
- exhibit the strengths of each participant's abilities
- encourage community building among students, teachers, and parents
- encourage reflection about controversial issues
- culminate in a meaningful center to explore complex questions
- demonstrate an integration of ideas and skills

- demonstrate creative and original work
- lead to further interactions among students, teachers, and community members

Ideas for Other Centers

Any topic can form the basis of the unit. Other units focused on such themes as change, power, and light. Students, teachers, and community collaborated on these units as they had on the Brazil unit. In each unit, students used brain-based approaches, and so their test scores improved in all disciplines related to the projects they created for centers.

In order to model multicultural cooperation, your students could study and compare one topic or area across three countries in each center. Students could display their work and interact with community members. They might illustrate international cuisine or music in self-published recipe books or CDs, which can then be sold to raise money for the event.

Including Three Countries at Each Center

If your group decides to incorporate three countries in each center, your questions will differ from the ones listed for Brazil. Questions might include some of the following:

1. How does each of these countries contribute to other parts of the world?
2. Describe and compare a musical event in each country.
3. In which country would you prefer to live as a teen? Why?
4. How can you represent these countries using any art form?
5. List three similarities among these countries. List three differences.
6. How does family life differ among these cultures?
7. How would people from each country enjoy life in the other two countries?
8. How would a typical menu in one country differ from menus in the other countries?

Displaying Work for the Community

How do you display the work in a meaningful way? Busy teachers and students sometimes fear the extra work that such a display could require. We found that it helped to begin our project with the display and community involvement as two of our goals. Rather than viewing our evening presentation as icing on a cake-baking exercise, it was part of the exercise itself. Students used their original plans to prepare the displays and involved their parents from the beginning. Everybody helped to make the final display a huge success.

We reserved the gym for a Thursday and Friday in order to set up the centers for a Friday night display. Afterward, a large crew of parents and students remained behind to clean up so that the gym could be used for physical education classes on Monday.

Such an evening promotes understanding of the cultures and allows students from a variety of backgrounds to display their strengths and heritage. This project invariably brings the community together and promotes understanding among people of varying backgrounds.

Celebrating Student Learning

Once centers are completed and the class has shared with one another, you could choose some aspect of each center to present in an evening of readings, dance, and music from Brazil. The student-prepared Brazilian cuisine and coffee will be a hit on such an evening. You could use classrooms with one or two centers displayed in each.

Within such a project, many opportunities can be found for students to teach others in the community. This exercise promotes an understanding and appreciation of various cultures, and also helps students to value differences among themselves.

After such an evening, one group started an interactive newsletter so that parents and students could write letters to the editor about their impressions. To avoid any embarrassment, students chose to make their letters anonymous. They wrote *Dear Mom, Dear Dad,* or *Dear Mom and Dad* rather than using names. Likewise, parents wrote *Dear Son* or *Dear Daughter* in response. Interactions in this newsletter showed students' and parents' enthusiasm for community projects. Students and parents spoke fondly of their work together, and many suggested this kind of project should be ongoing throughout high school.

Videotaping and Storing the Project

Some students enjoyed videotaping and benefited from an opportunity to videotape our centers. The photography teacher helped these students. They received credit in that elective for their work. In the process of filming, students learned to write commentaries for the displays, interview student workers, splice film, and create a quality video that would be acceptable to people in the community.

Students shared the videos with the rest of the class. They also showed the videos at a regular morning assembly so the school could enjoy Brazil as it was seen and represented through the eyes of grade 10 students. In addition, they offered the videos for sale to the community.

Publishing Short Stories, Essays, and Poetry about Brazil

Students formed a writing club as a result of the Brazil unit. In this club, students wrote stories and essays about Brazil. When they decided to publish their works, parents were invited to contribute. A few prominent writers in the community added their works to the students' works. As the centers grew in popularity, so did the publication. Teachers wrote their impressions of Brazil, and some artistic students added photographs and artwork of Brazil. A group of journalism students bound and published these works and sold them to parents and students as memoirs of their work together. They also placed copies in the library for other groups who were interested in Brazil. Students were pleased to see their work in print, and feedback was invaluable for these young writers.

Exchanging Ideas with a Class in Brazil

Students were especially interested in communicating with a grade 10 class in Brazil. This exchange was arranged through the Internet, and students e-mailed their messages and ideas back and forth. The exchange provided invaluable insights to both sides about cultural differences and interests.

Students checked with Brazilian students before including ideas in the centers. This practice added authenticity to the final works. Students enjoyed this communication and benefited from the insights they gained. Some described the e-mail exercise as the most valuable component of the project.

Although the exchange worked well for most students, some complained about the differences in sex roles across cultures, which led several female students to raise the issue of competition, hierarchical power, dominance, and conflict resolution across cultures.

We decided to use the roundtable approach to discuss gender issues and education in Brazil and other countries. One student raised the possibility that North American education is biased toward males. The issue created such a heated debate that all agreed we should research the topic and come together at a later date to discuss it.

DEVELOPING A GENDER-APPROPRIATE LEARNING ENVIRONMENT

The gender exercise caused us to think through an issue that had never before arisen in our class. Students worked in groups to identify their key concerns. Our discussion moved from research to heated debates to compiling a gender-appropriate checklist for our work. We posted the checklist as a reminder to include both genders in our own work together.

- We've taken various approaches to solve each problem.

- Both sexes were equally represented in discussions and original plans.

- An equal number of final ideas came from females and males.

- Females benefited in several ways from our work.

- Males benefited in several ways from our work.

- We used gender-neutral language.

- We made related technology available to both sexes.

- We adequately addressed biases related to past work.

- We promoted active listening, especially between sexes.

- We came to a better understanding of the sexes during the project.

- We provided opportunities to reflect on our progress in creating a gender-neutral environment.

Our debates and discussions improved communication between the sexes in each group and ensured that everyone participated freely within an accepting environment. One student found evidence from an Internet research site to show how females and males brains differ. From recent research, he showed how males tend to demonstrate more math proficiency, spatial ability and aggression, while female brain capabilities tend to orient toward language, emotion, and nurture. This student's illustrations enthused many students, who wanted to talk more about brains and gender differences, and the exchange that followed sent many students back to the library to find answers. A knowledgeable person in the community, who wrote about brain-based applications, was invited in as a facilitator for several student conversations. The depth of students' learning was triggered by their own curiosity; this in itself is a brain-based tactic that works well in secondary school and beyond. This tactic is too often ignored when lectures take center stage.

Discovering facts about brains led students into discussions about gender differences. Most agreed that both genders are needed for key decisions in class. Eager to know more about gender differences, students invited a parent who had a neuroscience background to class for a discussion on the topic of how brain differences impact on gender. Not only did the discussion help students to value differences across genders, but students were more eager to work together since they felt validated by the opposite sex. The speaker showed students how connectors tend to crisscross both sides of women's brains in ways that help them to integrate ideas and include relationships, while men's corpus callosum connects in a way to focus them deeply on one task at a time.

One volunteer in class told of her part-time job at the local mall and her feelings of intimidation because of gender expectations. Rather than put herself down, as she had when she was put in charge of older sales personnel, students suggested several brain-based solutions to help bring people together at work.

Pointing out gender distinctions in no way implies that all men are alike; nor does it assume that all women think in the same way. In fact, the opposite is true. Furthermore, since the human brain "rewires" each night as people sleep, their brains are constantly changing. The mall employee offered answers she found for working with basic differences in people to bring about more respect.

Through roundtable problem solving, students became aware of differences between the sexes and felt free to express their personal frustrations about what they saw as abuse and to offer suggestions for equality. As a result, they grew to understand, appreciate, and gradually to affirm one another. They celebrated their unique qualities as responses to shared problems or contributions to community projects. They also enjoyed the fact that intelligence is not fixed as once thought and that they can grow new dendrite brain cells in any intelligence just through using their brains in tasks that draw in that intelligence. "You mean, we can actually get smarter?" one senior asked. The answer is a definite yes. In a brain-compatible class, students can grow new dendrites daily as they encourage one another to reach for and attain higher results. Circles that discuss together how this can happen have happier teens who enjoy higher achievement.

ACTIVITY 2.1 Questions Work Best in Safe Environments

Outcome
A description of how three students will use the eight ways of knowing to contribute to a final product

Discussion and Procedure

Have students brainstorm to find and share one key question that their projects will attempt to answer. They will decide how many of Gardner's ways of knowing they can incorporate into their project, using a chart to outline their ideas. Each person might be responsible for bringing two ways of knowing to the presentation. They will go over the whole project to make sure they incorporate all eight ways of knowing into a well-organized presentation. Remind them that all sections of the presentation should be a response to one overall question.

ACTIVITY 2.2   Shared Activities

Outcome

A list of helpful materials to be shared across several disciplines

Discussion and Procedure

A unit such as the one described in this chapter may be overwhelming for one teacher to prepare. But in a roundtable, communities form around one common goal. For the Brazil unit, teachers might form one community. This activity could shape a roundtable approach.

Each teacher shares one activity that develops at least one skill that may be useful to another teacher. Teachers provide sketches or handouts of these activities or materials. They discuss the relevance for the activity in each of the classes to provide insights from a variety of perspectives. They share individual and immediate needs for activities or materials in specific areas. Others in the group volunteer ideas or provide handouts that respond to each request. For example, a social studies teacher might hand out an essay outline form. The outline may be useful for students who have difficulty organizing their notes and rough drafts into well-written essays.

ACTIVITY 2.3   Create a Book for a Young Friend

Outcome

A personalized book for a younger child

Discussion and Procedure

Learning communities can reach across grades and interests. With a teacher of a grade lower than yours, arrange suitable times and places for your students to meet in pairs. Invite each of your students to choose one name from a class list of the younger children. Your students will interview the younger ones to gather information and ideas about learning preferences and stories they enjoy. They will use a predesigned set of interview questions or will prepare their own questions. The following might be useful interview questions:

1. What stories do you like best?

2. Tell me about your best friend.

3. Describe pets you enjoy.

4. What games do you like to play?

5. What frightens you?

6. What makes you laugh?

7. What makes you cry?

8. Tell me about your family.

9. What do you enjoy most at school? What do you enjoy least?

The students then will write the younger students' responses on questionnaires to be used for reference. The older students will visit the children's section of the library and study the illustrations and plots of books that children most enjoy. They will also research how the younger children's interests relate to some aspect of a topic that was chosen by your students for this project.

In groups of three or four, students will brainstorm the parts of a children's book. The idea is to personalize some part of the topic and relate it to interests the younger child expressed. Writers might choose Brazilian animals, food, or sports. In the younger child's class, read the stories and present the books to the appropriate children. Share snacks and have several of the stories read to the entire group.

ACTIVITY 2.4   Tips for Making an Enjoyable Family Activity

Outcome

A list of tips for making a successful and joyful family activity

Discussion and Procedure

This activity will ensure more success in the creation of family-centered community. Generate a list of ten tips for planning a successful and joyful family activity. Make a similar list for a family in the unit you are studying. Have students interview family members for their ideas for the list. Create a mock interview of someone in the culture or from the country you are studying. You may wish to talk to parents or siblings on audio- or videotape, using the tape as your notes. Feel free to use humor as you write out the list of ten steps to take for your chosen activity.

Go over your completed list with other family members to check for details left out or added incorrectly. Ask family members to check your research on lifestyles of people from the culture you are studying. With another student, read and edit your rough drafts.

Your list may resemble the list below, which illustrates ten tips for successful car buying.

1. List exactly your needs, your wants, and the preferred model. Decide exactly what you can afford and stay within that limit. How will your preferences compare to those of a Brazilian family?

2. Study the price books. Determine your trade-in estimate plus the discount you hope to negotiate. Tell your banker what you want and ask how you can get a fair price. How do prices compare in Brazil?

3. Be prepared to compare. Don't feel pressured into a fast sale. Shop around for the equipment you want at the price you can afford. What are the buying and selling habits in Brazil?

4. Ask questions. Talk openly about what you want and don't allow yourself to be intimidated or manipulated. How do Brazilians communicate in sales situations?

5. Inspect the car thoroughly. Don't settle for just a look. Take the car for a test drive, using various speeds and maneuvers. Compare to car inspections in Brazil.

6. Negotiate wisely. Get away from the deal emotionally. Go for a walk; talk it over with a friend before buying. Don't let pretty frills or shiny extras influence your final decision. Do Brazilians negotiate when they buy cars?

7. Write the agreement out. You, not the salesperson, should control the deal—this is your money. If you cannot get what you feel is a good deal, ask to speak to the manager or simply leave and go to another car dealer. What would a Brazilian contract look like?

8. Anticipate the salesperson's objections. Be prepared for a higher price and lower trade-in offer. Justify your position, present your evidence, use strategies. How does one argue for a lower price in Brazil?

9. Don't exceed your present limits. It is better to take another day to consider than to make a bad decision. What factors must a Brazilian buyer consider here?

10. Double-check everything. Use your own calculator to check all the figures. Read all small print. Finally, reinspect your car just before you take delivery. Happy driving! What overall differences and similarities do Brazilians experience?

ACTIVITY 2.5　Project Planning Sheet for Negotiated Assessment

Outcome
Student-created planning sheet to select a title for a project and to summarize the topic, guiding question, aim, materials required, and evaluation criteria

Discussion and Procedure
Communities are shaped by working together on common goals. Roundtable activities may be projects (such as Brazilian lifestyles) or activities for negotiating assessment. Assessment activities could be planning criteria on which to assess a project, the creation of student portfolios, or creation of a puppet show to demonstrate understanding of a concept.

This activity draws assessment ideas into the main activity and helps students view assessment as an integral part of the learning process. This activity may be done collaboratively with the teacher, with peers or with parents, or it may be completed individually.

Each student writes the title for the project on a sheet of paper. He adds his name and class on the next line. He writes the interdisciplinary topic for which the project is assigned. He creates one main guiding question, which he will answer or pose in the project. This question should be tightly stated and should be addressed in every aspect of the assignment.

He states briefly his aim or what he hopes this project will accomplish. He lists all materials required to complete the project, including texts, magazines, colored paper, VCR, tape recorders, and so on. In point form, he lists the evaluation criteria for which he would like to be evaluated. Criteria may include the following:

creative ideas	relationship to the curriculum topic
original thought	spelling and sentence structure
good research	use of all eight ways of knowing
organization	relationship to the student's real world

ACTIVITY 2.6 Let Puppets Tell the Story

Outcome
A puppet show that responds to one aspect of an issue

Discussion and Procedure
As students help plan the assessment process, they gain a more complete understanding of their goals and focus. Students can demonstrate clear understanding of new material in many ways. For example, a puppet show may provide opportunities for students to work together in order to experience new ideas, critique textbook information, and make judgments about written content.

Each person writes down one personally probing question from the lesson. This question may concern any aspect of the topic. In groups of five, students choose one question and figure out how to address it through a puppet show. Students brainstorm ideas for a play that involves at least five puppets. They could write the play together, or each one could choose a scene to write in rough form and have the group edit it. Students prepare the final story on paper and practice the puppet show.

To prepare the show, students first brainstorm for physical and personality traits of each puppet and then use classroom materials to create the puppets. They prepare the final script and practice, using the classroom puppet theater. They might decide to build their own theater or get parents involved in the process. They choose a date and time to present the puppet shows to the class and perhaps later to the community.

ACTIVITY 2.7 Fishbone Graphic Organizer

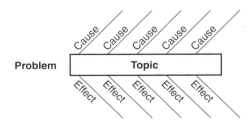

Outcome
A fishbone graphic organizer or thinking sheet that investigates cause and effect

Discussion and Procedure
Roundtable assessment projects may begin simply, by using something like a fishbone graphic organizer to brainstorm new ideas. In groups of four or five, students create fishbone charts

to show the causes and effects of some significant aspects of the lesson. At the head of the fishbone, they state the problem. They brainstorm ideas for five causes of the problems, writing these causes on the fins. They list several effects of each cause. They write the title or topic across the spine of the fishbone.

MOTIVATIONAL TOOLS THAT BUILD CLASSES INTO COMMUNITIES

To make motivation a daily part of students' work helps keep them on track for positive life changes that will serve them far beyond any class. Below are several brain-based tips to ensure that their motivational toolboxes are ready to enhance each activity they undertake. Invite students to show how they will do each of the following as they begin a new project.

1. Start with your own abilities and work within your limitations. Any contributions you make to this community will come back to you in valuable resources you can take into any enterprise. List your abilities on one side of a paper and your limitations on the other side. Dare to think in bigger and better dimensions and illustrate ways to dwell on successes rather than focus on failures.

2. Try changing your approach to a difficult activity. When you give up on a difficult task, your mind gives up trying to help you succeed. Remember to think about the results you want to achieve, and your mind will guide you to higher outcomes.

3. Stay committed to the group in projects. People have a tendency to look around for a better group of people to work with. Lack of personal commitment to a group is the greatest cause for failure in that group. Get committed and learn to say yes to anything that will promote excellence in the group's outcomes. Be your own person, and invite others to give their best so that differences are valued as part of the whole.

4. Refuse to allow setbacks in your group to control you, and help the group members stick to their plans for success. Don't be intimidated when you see others do well in another group; instead congratulate them and mean it. When you face disappointments in your group, do more than take notice—take action to fix key problems and move the team forward. Challenge others to new creative possibilities for growth together each time the group meets. Surprise and delight your team by an offering you bring to the group that uses a talent you sometimes forget to use.

Since motivation provides the glue that holds successful communities together, it will be worth the practice and perseverance required to keep it flowing daily. Use these tips weekly to keep spirits high and goals on track, and you'll inspire the positive energy it takes to succeed together in any team.

CHAPTER 3

The Roundtable Approach to Identifying Unique Abilities

It takes a whole village to raise a child.

African proverb

When faculty identify and appreciate their own gifts, they usually contribute to nurturing vibrant communities. In this chapter, you will find MITA tools for identifying what makes each person "tick." You will also encounter myths that tend to prevent brain-friendly communities, as well as tips to nurture learning by building on student differences.

Consider the following ten misconceptions and realities listed below and identify how each one impacts your learning community. Since students' success is impacted by their beliefs about their brains, you may want to explore these misconceptions with your students.

MISCONCEPTIONS ABOUT OUR BRAINS AND SUCCESSFUL OPPORTUNITIES

Unfortunately, many students and faculty have limited facts about their mental possibilities, which often leads to feelings of failure for secondary or college students. These feelings result in limited success and can also lead to emotional problems such as stress or depression. To help identify misconceptions and misunderstandings about the brain's optimum capabilities, students require current information about their brains.

1. **Misconception:** "I'm not as smart as others I know, and that's why I succeed less."

Reality: Intelligence is not fixed as we once believed it was. Biological research tells us that our brainpower expands with challenges. Brains are "hardwired" to unscramble complex puzzles and provide answers to even unfamiliar problems, and yet too few find out how this growth occurs.

2. **Misconception:** "In school, others always outshone me, and now it's too late to achieve high goals."

Reality: Some people think their opportunities have passed by and now it is too late to grow and succeed. This is an unfortunate fact, because they do not realize that their limiting thoughts will create limited results. When we challenge each of our intelligences, we grow new connecting brain cells called dendrites; this helps us achieve in multiple ways. Well into our senior years, we can grow smarter in spite of age, background, or educational foundation.

3. **Misconception:** "Self-disciplined people do not fail as much as I do."

Reality: Self-disciplined people, like everyone else, get tired or sick at times and also fail. Chemicals called neurotransmitters seep through clefts in our brains and convert to electrical impulses. This electrical and chemical activity affects our emotions and impacts learning. This activity can be altered in a variety of ways, including relaxation techniques or aromatherapy, which can increase serotonin, or laughter sessions, which can stimulate positive enzymes.

4. **Misconception:** "If I worked harder and longer each day, I could get further ahead."

Reality: Some of the ways we work against rather than with our brains comes from the fact that we work harder and longer and sleep less. Sleep affects our mental progress, since our brains "rewire" completely each day as we sleep. Rewiring is based on the previous day's activity and relies on adequate amounts of deep sleep each night. So while unsuccessful people often work longer and harder, successful people know that more benefit is gained from consistent sleep than from longer work hours.

5. **Misconception:** "I am more the creative type, and I tend to "wing" things as I go."

Reality: Logical or mathematical intelligence is linked to creating detailed expectations, which often manifest in checklists or carefully crafted directions that prevent sloppy results. Creativity and careful expectations partner well to increase possibilities for success, and both are learned strategies. These two characteristics are not mutually exclusive, and one does not preclude the other. People who sustain success tell us that they tend to organize and plan for successful results. Many highly creative people use organizational strategies.

6. **Misconception:** "Others in my family are much smarter than I am."

Reality: We enjoy success because of the genes we are born with and also as a result of approaches and patterns that we learn through life. For instance, great questions influence achievement, since questions help us to increase curiosity and act more from a sense of wonder than from mere routines. Questions help us to prevent passivity that leads to failure. If you feel that others in your family are smarter, you may not be leading with your strengths. Each time you use your intelligences to create something or to solve problems, you can increase those intelligences. Regardless of what you are born with, you can increase your intellectual capacity through doing tasks such as those illustrated in this program.

7. **Misconception:** "I can't remember things anymore."

Reality: Memory is connected to how we store information, and we can learn to retrieve facts when we need them. When we link new ideas onto something we already know well, it is much easier to retrieve and use the new ideas later. People who have good memories have learned how to link ideas together so they can use these to solve real-life problems.

8. **Misconception:** "Little things bother me more than they bother others, and I can't help the fact that I worry more than most people."

Reality: We are never stuck in a place of worry without help. Our brains are miraculously flexible. Serotonin is a hormone that increases calm, contentment, and well-being. The hormone cortisol can lead us to panic and anxiety. We can influence both states by practicing ways to decrease or stimulate our hormone levels, such as recalling a memory or music we enjoy or having lunch with a good friend. In this way, we enrich our mental performance so that we thrive rather than fail.

9. **Misconception:** "I suffer from less energy than smarter people."

Reality: When we make health a priority in our lives, we also improve our mental health in significant ways. Success builds on success when it comes to mental growth, since human brains record and act on messages we file into its data banks. We can learn to enjoy every resource available to increase emotional, mental, and spiritual health. We can both nurture and sustain healthy brains for higher-quality lives through a few simple attitude changes and through storing positive plans.

10. **Misconception:** "My abilities seem less useful to my daily activity than people who can take their talents to class with them."

Reality: We can all engage our multiple intelligences to achieve more success. Through daily reflection, we build success from past failures. We can engage an unused intelligence to get past former problems in innovative new ways. For instance, you may be shy, but you play an instrument well. Music can help start your next conversation. You might invite a person you'd like to know better to hear a band. Then, during a walk home, you can discuss music and draw in the other person through a topic you enjoy. You have raised your comfort level, stimulated serotonin for calmness, and ignited a conversation that could lead to a good relationship.

We can engage our natural abilities when we imagine our full range of gifts, talents, and intelligences as unique tools to build a more successful life.

LEARNING AND TEACHING THROUGH MITA'S ROUNDTABLE PROCESS

A key question might be: *How can students identify and develop their individual gifts and abilities in class?* The MITA model involves solutions from teachers, students, and researchers in a community-building endeavor. It integrates the best practices you use and applies related learning approaches you have encountered in brain-based roundtables. The MITA process provides an integrated approach to community building that helps improve motivation and achievement for students. This process relates to three C's—collaboration, content, and criteria.

Collaboration

- Collaboration among teachers increases their resources.
- Inviting parents to share ideas draws on their support.
- Consulting with students offers them a new sense of purpose.

Content

- Brainstorming with students offers new insights into facts.
- Introducing brain-compatible tasks leads to deeper understanding.
- Integrating curriculum allows students to solve problems in the real world.

Criteria

- Negotiating assessment gives students specific rubrics as a guide to excellence.
- Presenting projects allows for applications that reinforce students' understanding.
- Videotaping projects creates a track record and provides benchmarks.

Using the MITA *Five Steps to Smart* Program (see Figure 0.1 on page 6) students, parents, and teachers can create roundtables for higher student achievement at school as they build on unique interests and draw on past experiences.

ASSESSMENT CRITERIA

As faculty brainstorm with students for acceptable assessment criteria, they help learners to create quality projects. In brain-friendly classes, criteria used by students to create their projects are the same criteria used by faculty to assess the project. Examples of such project criteria follow:

- Provide rich contexts as background to your topic.
- Relate your topic to life beyond school.
- Display knowledge about skills in and relating to an understanding of your topic.
- Exhibit your strengths using multiple intelligences demonstrations.
- Encourage cooperation among other students, parents, and teachers.
- Encourage a reflective stance on learning.
- Culminate in meaningful products.
- Demonstrate suitability for interdisciplinary work.
- Provide possibilities for original work.
- Lead to further interactions between other students, parents, and teachers.

Although many teachers use similar criteria for evaluating a project, fewer share these criteria with their students before the project is created. In brain-compatible classes, criteria are listed and applied so that students are aware of what is expected. Such core criteria can form the basics from which students and faculty create specific rubrics to guide any project. The following are examples of criteria used for evaluation of a project:

- conceptualization
- presentation

- quality (technique, originality, accuracy)

- individuality

- evidence of cooperativeness (working with others, use of various sources, and so on)

- coherence with curriculum topics

Students can add to this list their own expected assessment criteria. Such an approach to assessment makes it part of the overall learning process instead of treating it as a separate entity to be administered as a test at the end of each unit. Such performance-based assessment can indicate how well each student has mastered a task.

Intelligence-Fair Assessment

The goal is to make assessment more intelligence fair. The alternative tests and evaluation techniques that follow indicate more fairly each student's real progress. To do so, teachers and students assess topics in a variety of ways to make evaluation fair to all students. The following list may help teachers and students expand their assessment tools to include roundtable teaching in classroom communities.

- anecdotal records
- observational checklists
- portfolios
- written tests (multiple-choice, short-answer, essay)
- self-evaluations
- oral presentations
- student projects
- interviews
- student-led conferences
- journals, logs, diaries
- videotapes
- tape recordings
- criterion-referenced evaluations
- performances
- peer evaluations
- extended problem-solving projects
- homework
- take-home tests
- joint goal setting
- summative categories
- formative categories
- inventories, attitude, interest, learning styles
- evaluation standards, achievement tests

Videotaping Projects

As a means of documenting and assessing students' work and progress, you can collect each student's projects throughout the school year and include them in a classroom library. Some students enjoy creating videos, photographs, and slides. You can file videotapes as part of the assessment and also as a record of each stage. Students can create digital videos to display their work in student-led conferences presented to the community at a later date.

THE MITA COMMUNITY-BUILDING APPROACH

The MITA community-building approach originated through an exchange of ideas with parents, students, and teachers about learning and teaching. According to Hargreaves and others (Hargreaves and Fullen, 1992), schools and universities are traditionally set up for learning in isolation. We continue to see negative results from this learning environment in terms of students ability to use more of their capabilities to enhance their learning.

UCLA's Higher Education Research Institute (2000) surveyed more than 260,000 full-time college freshmen, who reported boredom, drudgery, and disengagement in class. There is a growing need for practical approaches to change the culture of passivity and isolation that permeates higher education. This book highlights several reasons for this lack of interest in secondary and higher education, but the main focus is to provide a practical model to address and help resolve this problem. The practices provided in the next section came from efforts to engage students in multiple ways in a freshman university class.

BUILDING A CARING COMMUNITY IN A UNIVERSITY CLASS

Most would agree that community is defined differently. Scientists define community in one way, churches define it in another. For this book's purpose, *community* is a group of unique, gifted individuals who bond with one another and hold a set of shared values that they use to respond to problems and to address

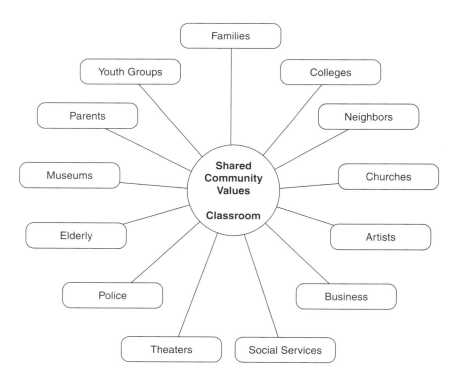

common questions. In brain-friendly communities, bonding is tight enough to provide meaningful social and educational relationships but loose enough to accommodate a variety of approaches to solving the most complex problems.

To say that no one recipe exists for building community does not imply that communities just happen. They do not. Neither are they simply willed into existence. Our collective determination to build community and the group's desire to practice community learning create a gradual unity, wherein individuals show they care about others through a tone that values ideas they hear and through the safety that allows for stating ideas and insights in front of the group. Each group takes on a special identity, and each group shares a sense of belonging as members interact and use their multiple intelligences to explore the ideas being taught. The result over time is a sense of family and a dedicated commitment to work things out.

Communities require planning. They don't just spring up like mushrooms, but neither do they wither when the heat comes. Over the past quarter century, I have built communities in high school classes, among business leaders, and among teachers-in-training on university campuses. Students often complain that universities lack caring communities, so we decided to investigate this complaint and explore what would make a healthy learning community among teachers. The practical tips and tools in this book can help you build community within a variety of age groups and backgrounds.

Our purpose was to transform lecture hall teaching into an interactive roundtable approach at a university in Toronto. The MITA model was applied to demonstrate how this would work for teachers-in-training. The project involved forty-six teachers-in-training and one lecturer-in-training in a class on models of teaching at York University in Toronto. Students in this class already held at least one degree, and many were experts in demanding careers. Together we agreed to explore the notion of roundtable learning during our one-year course. We raised issues about the isolation that often exists in higher education. We discussed possible answers to such questions as "How does roundtable learning operate?" "How does it differ from traditional teacher-in-charge learning?" "Who does what?"

Changing the paradigm, we agreed, would change the classroom atmosphere. Classrooms that changed from top-down, teacher-controlled formats into vibrant roundtable communities would help create a caring community. We moved from a hierarchical system to a circle of fellow colleagues. New roles moved students and teacher to maximize their learning, since each would become both student and teacher. The changed rules and roles pressed our group toward further change.

In our roundtable community, we were challenged to interact and at times were dependent on one another's expertise. Rather than teacher controls, our community relied on professional socialization and collegiality and welcomed interdependence for leadership. We shared decisions about curriculum design, assignments, and assessment practices. As the class progressed, we interacted not only through shared decision making, but also through a general caring about one another's welfare and success. In Gardner's terms, we were developing our interpersonal intelligence.

After only three weeks, we began to enjoy the affirmation of shared values. We valued knowledge for its own sake and trusted our abilities to apply ideas, test their validity in real-life situations, and share the results with the group on a regular basis. In many cases, the circle opened as members shared their responses and investigations.

Does this scenario sound like a typical high school or university class? Likely it does not. When we decided to create community, we looked for models of community among faculty and within classrooms. We had to define clearly what we wanted from a roundtable community before we could become one. We talked about building collegiality, ensuring responsibilities, and sharing values.

Collegiality, we decided, comes more from within than from a list of correlates to implement. To change from a hierarchical system to a community requires mutual obligations as well as emotional and normative ties. In order to change the paradigm, we first had to create our own community criteria, identify our shared values, and instill our professional norms and practices.

We needed to translate abstract ideas about community building into practice and seek ways to introduce more relational activities. Many of these curriculum activities are provided in this book.

Facilitating Community

After exploring some possibilities for building community, members of a different English methods class and I consciously decided to build a strong learning community during our term together. The idea was to identify patterns that would help us build communities with students of every age.

In roundtable, we learned together. In collaboration, we solved academic problems and developed quality curriculum based on our research questions. We asked the question "How can a teacher facilitate community in the classroom?" We broke into groups to consider the community qualities we would emphasize. Each group chose to examine community through one of the following topics:

- classroom management
- collaborative learning
- community involvement
- learning obstacles
- quality curriculum
- lifelong learning

We asked the question "How does each topic influence community building within an intermediate classroom?" To answer this question, we drew on one another's knowledge and wisdom. First, we identified our personal skills and abilities, using Gardner's multiple intelligences theory and my MITA model. We identified Gardner's eight ways of knowing by listing our preferred ways of knowing. We named skills in which we were accomplished or hobbies we enjoyed. To value all abilities and interests, we decided, would be to build community. We included abilities and interests in language, mathematics, music, athletics, art, interpersonal relationships, and personal reflection skills.

At this point, we formed six diverse groups. Each group had one person with strengths in the mathematical-logical intelligence; each had a person with strengths in the musical-rhythmic intelligence; and so on. Together we listed possible activities for each identified ability. Since most of us were humanities majors, we agreed to help one another fill in the math gaps and to respond to Gardner's eight ways of knowing. First, we completed Campbell, Campbell, and Dickinson's (1992) interest inventory. The interest inventory increased our awareness of our own unique abilities and goals and also made us aware of one another's strengths and weaknesses. Second, we questioned how a strong community functions. M. Scott Peck (1988) maintains that strong communities of any kind are realistic enough for people to speak their minds and buck the trends but still safe enough to allow limitations without fear of rejection. We agreed that community welcomes people's gifts and abilities and does not exclude ideas or ideologies that are different from the teacher's.

In other words, community would require us to hang in when the going got rough and to celebrate human differences rather than ignore, hide, or try to change them. Peck concludes that while the word *community* is bandied about frequently, few genuine communities exist in reality. We agreed that in most of our classes, community was often obstructed by such forces as rigid competition, power struggles, intolerance, and misunderstandings. Students also suggested that they sometimes felt powerless to change what had traditionally been a teacher's, rather than a community, arena.

Lieberman (1992) calls for communities that bridge between university and lower-level schools. She recommends a bridge between teachers and students. Building better bridges between universities and schools, between research and practice, requires a shift from top-down dictates to more group consensus. In community, we each have unique talents to offer as well as much to learn. In the University of Toronto class, for instance, we worked as a group to solve most problems. Students and instructor exchanged roles as each contributed and learned. As a preliminary to our roundtable community, we first agreed to level the traditional fences between university instructor and teachers-in-training. Respect for one another grew as our highest common denominator. We welcomed new ideas and learning strategies from the group. By choosing to make these deliberate structural changes, we moved away from the teacher-centered system to build a new structure that represented our shared culture. We moved continually from theory to practice in building this culture.

Our learning did not come without a few misunderstandings and struggles to find out who was responsible for what. As instructor, I failed more than my students. On the coldest Monday morning of the term, for instance, I grew frustrated with many students who arrived late. The students had valid excuses. (Some had been on the freeways into Toronto for several hours.) But rather than comment on the fact that not one student stayed home that day, I gave a minilecture on the importance of promptness in any class. My response was inconsistent with roundtable philosophy. So I apologized to the class, and the subsequent discussion considered roles and expectations.

Roles and Role Expectations

Our third step was to ask, "Who does what in vibrant learning communities?" We traded the traditional idea of teacher-in-charge for a collection of learners with a shared vision. In other words, we saw ourselves on lifelong journeys where we looked to one another for ideas about curriculum content, subject specialties, and strategies for teaching English content. With the basic premise of "learners in fellowship," we set out to identify critical questions we would ask. We set up forums through which we could express and exchange ideas. We discussed key questions, invited guest speakers, shared films, presented ideas in small groups, created an e-mail newsgroup, and wrote personal reflections.

In one sense we became a group of experts with strong individuality, but in another sense we acknowledged our interdependence, and not only in intellectual exchanges. We accepted alternative emotional and spiritual differences, seeking to relate more than superficially from the very depths of our hearts. The idea here was that "only as we bring to learning more of who we are, including our past experiences, our faith, and our unique talents, can we take away more of who we hope to become" (Weber 1996, p. v).

Fostering a Community of Learners

Finally, we asked how teachers can foster communities of learners. School communities are natural conduits for learning cooperatively and for problem solving. The question is "How can busy teachers can create strong, caring communities on an everyday basis?" One answer came to me from the high Arctic. I observed that Inuit communities traditionally involve diverse people as they work toward common goals. Inuit communities emphasize commonalties, celebrate diversities, and do not concentrate on divisions, so people are energized. We built a learning community based on these values. The activities in this chapter can provide models for you and your students as you build teaching and learning communities.

ACTIVITY 3.1   Goal Setting with Parents, Students, and Teachers

Outcome
A weekly or monthly record of goals and progress

Discussion and Procedure
Students keep a weekly or monthly record, with input from parents and teachers regarding their progress. Have students use a form that covers the eight intelligences to set goals and record their progress in several ways of knowing. Start simply. The following list and questions will help students determine what kinds of activities represent each intelligence and what their strengths are.

1. Musical-rhythmic—includes singing, playing an instrument, culture

2. Bodily-kinesthetic—includes gymnastics, sports, running, dancing, coordination and building activities

3. Visual-spatial—includes visual arts, sculpting, crafts, geometry, interior decorating

4. Verbal-linguistic—includes reading, writing, poetry, stories, debates, speeches, media phrases

5. Mathematical-logical—includes math, visual work, organization, problem solving, sequencing ideas, thinking logically

6. Interpersonal—includes relationships with others, respect, multicultural understanding, helping others solve problems

7. Intrapersonal—includes self-confidence, self-management, values, spiritual truths, reflections

8. Naturalistic—includes use of nature to analyze, categorize, describe, compare, and collect evidences

Questions
What goals will you concentrate on most?
What goals will you work on next?

| **ACTIVITY 3.2** | **Creating a Family Tree and History** |

Outcome

An understanding of the student's family's genealogy

Discussion and Procedure

Students discuss with their parents and other family members what is known about family members. They use a computer program or illustrations to position each known member of their families on a family group record. They identify what they want to know about the family members: Where and when were they born? Where and when did they die? What occupation did they have? Were they married? What talents, abilities, and training did they have? What personality traits? They should find out the answers to as many questions as they can. They may wish to obtain some information in the library, which has good sources for tracing genealogies. They can obtain other knowledge from relatives. They may have to write to distant relatives, but they can compile many stories from these exchanges.

Using a particular objective for each process, they chart and illustrate the family in a variety of ways in order to share information they gather. They may tape some interviews or assemble samples of projects completed by different family members to create a display. They may chart their own history and show which relatives they are most like and which they least resemble. With members of their families, they will decide how to organize and share the information and then present a proposal to the teacher stating what questions they researched, how they obtained information, which family members worked with them, and how they plan to present and share the information.

| **ACTIVITY 3.3** | **Reflection Sheets** |

Outcome

Reflection sheets that enable students to reflect on their past experiences and express their prior knowledge

Discussion and Procedure

When we brainstorm and ask questions to identify students' abilities and interests, we validate their offerings. An interest inventory helps students reflect on their strengths and identify weaknesses or concerns. Regular dialogues and student-teacher conferences require teachers to assume the role of guide or facilitator more than that of teacher, and teaching takes on exciting new dimensions. The following teaching techniques can be used in a roundtable community-building approach:

- guided student discovery through hands-on activities

- modeling of how to enjoy a learning activity

- brainstorming with students, other teachers, and parents

- advanced organizers to show overview of new work

- questioning students and having them question others

- small-group work, including shared inquiry and peer teaching

- conferencing with students

- student presentations, teacher presentation, lectures
- strong visuals to describe stages of the lesson
- experience charts to show a student's relationship to the topics
- games and simulations, often created by students
- computer-assisted instruction
- centers that students create for eight ways of knowing a topic
- experimentation and investigation
- performances, role-plays, and theatrical techniques
- practice and application activities that use multiple intelligences
- field trips and community involvement
- creative problem solving
- independent studies and research projects
- semantic mapping and related discussions
- offering choices so that students design or choose their projects
- portfolios that show one month's progress
- writing to learn, learning logs
- interest and ability inventories for each topic
- building background for a story or narrating a play
- exploratory talk and discussion
- problem solving in groups and individually
- transformation from one form to another
- cooperative learning in groups of three
- observation activities in which students observe and report back
- use of audiovisuals to report learning
- constructing dioramas or mock-ups on the topic
- building manipulatives to show resolutions
- visualizations and imagery to reflect on information

When teachers employ a wider variety of approaches in their teaching, students can employ more ways of knowing any lesson. A few reflection questions before any unit raise students' awareness of new material to be learned. Questions can help students become aware of barriers to learning. Questions can probe their thinking to increase curiosity and motivation. The following are samples of reflection questions you might ask your students before a unit on poetry.

What does poetry mean to you?

In what ways might poetry influence your life?

Do you enjoy writing poetry? Why or why not?

Did you enjoy reading poetry in the past? Why or why not?

How would you read a great poem to the class?

ACTIVITY 3.4   Introducing MI Theory to Students

Outcome
A collage showing Gardner's eight ways of knowing

Discussion and Procedure
According to Gardner (1991), intelligences are always expressed in the context of specific tasks, domains, and disciplines. To introduce Gardner's learning approaches, invite students to create a large collage demonstrating multiple intelligences.

Students enjoy working in groups to create a collage. The activity serves to remind them of the various domains. As they cut, paste, and design, they will discuss their own learning proclivities and ask questions about how they can address each ability in their own projects.

1. **Mathematical-logical**—Students might show scientists and mathematical instruments, or chess players who use long chains of reasoning to solve problems.

2. **Verbal-linguistic**—Students might show speakers and poets and include journalism samples. Many symbols show sensitivity to the sounds, rhythms, and meanings of words and the various functions of language.

3. **Musical-rhythmic**—Students might illustrate music composition and use photographs of well-known bands. This section could also show pictures of music students who appreciate rhythm, pitch, and timbre, as well as a variety of forms of musical expressiveness.

4. **Visual-spatial**—Students might include information about an Arctic navigator; sculptures, art, and architecture; a variety of graph displays; or a large map of the world.

5. **Bodily-kinesthetic**—Students might portray dancers, athletes, or students using manipulatives to build objects.

6. **Interpersonal**—Students might show therapists, salespersons, politicians, media personnel, and union leaders.

7. **Intrapersonal**—Students might portray an array of reflective people, such as Gandhi, Martin Luther King Jr., Mother Teresa, and a psychology student.

8. **Naturalistic**—Students might show plants, natural museums, rock collections, natural disasters, human-made patterns and shapes, art from nature.

ACTIVITY 3.5   Creating a Sharp Focus in Photography

Students express their personal interests through use of photography and artistic displays.

Outcome
A collage or poster made up of photographs of hobbies and interests, emphasizing a sharp focus in both the photographs and the written captions

Discussion and Procedure

The key question in this activity is *How can a mandated high school or college curriculum be covered in a variety of ways without adding extra work for students?* A thematic or integrated approach should not put students at any disadvantage. Nor should it add to faculty's workload.

You might consider mandated curriculum topics as springboards to a deeper understanding of the topic rather than as ends in themselves. Activities and projects to explore the curriculum reach beyond any one way of knowing and include many of the activities in the brainstormed list. Integration can take many forms. This activity provides an example of how a teacher may start.

Discuss with students the importance of a sharp focus—to present one clear idea—both in photography and in writing. Brainstorm for factors that result in fuzzy photos. List factors that cause fuzzy writing (for example, too many details crammed into one essay or a lack of transitions). Have students limit their projects to a few of their greatest interests and abilities. Have them ask themselves "What details will contribute directly to my topic?" "Which unrelated details should be omitted?" They then write their main ideas for their projects and list materials they will require. They may wish to involve family members in their projects and invite them to take pictures and help organize the display. They will title their posters or displays.

They then examine the photographs and the captions for a sharp focus and relevant message. They should ask for advice from others before completing their layouts. They should consider using satire or humor in their projects, if it is appropriate, and art or graphics to complete the display. They add captions under each photo, using as few words as possible to explain the scene. Remind them to eliminate all unnecessary words, keeping only strong or descriptive words. They then show their displays to the class. They might hang the displays on the bulletin boards for a parents' evening.

ACTIVITY 3.6 Celebrating Peer Differences and Similarities

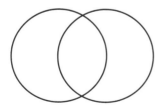

Outcome

A Venn diagram of students' differences and similarities

Discussion and Procedure

Have students pair up and brainstorm interests and abilities related to the topic. They list differences (different opinions, talents, interests, and abilities) that each brings to the project. They list things related to the topic and abilities they have in common. Using a Venn diagram, they list their major differences in sections to the left and right. They list similarities and things they agree on in the center section. They brainstorm ways in which each partner might help the other during the unit and then choose at least five ways in which they can work together as partners to help each other learn the material.

Join two pairs of students and have them compare Venn diagrams. Have them add any areas in which a student with strengths in one area can help one who is weaker in that area. Consider the strengths of the team of four. Students select a project for the unit being studied that might use the strengths of their group and that will strengthen the weaker areas.

| ACTIVITY 3.7 | Gathering Books for the Class Library |

Outcome

A classroom library of books or magazines on upcoming topics

Discussion and Procedure

Given the dwindling public purse, we must find resources within strong communities to ensure equitable opportunities for education. The quality of learning can be enhanced when interested parents and families contribute one or two books to form a classroom library. Over the years, these resources grow and so do students' opportunities to do quality research.

Discuss the projects that students might do. Ask students what books they would like to read on each topic. Make a list of all the topics and send this list to the parents. Ask parents and students to donate one or two books on these topics. You might also arrange for a local bookstore to bring in a display of appropriate books that parents could purchase at a discount.

| ACTIVITY 3.8 | Compiling an Activity Bank |

Outcome

A file folder, book, or computer disk of activities organized into sections, with one title assigned for each topic

Discussion and Procedure

Teacher communities can also share resources in order to benefit from one another's ideas and also to avoid duplication of materials. Teacher helpers compile your shared activities under topics or titles so that you create a bank of useful activities. Find a good, central location to store the activity bank, such as in the library or as part of an audiovisual collection. Wherever materials are stored, the bank's success will depend on maintaining accurate records so that teachers know who has materials at any time as well as the time and date activities are expected back in the bank.

All teachers would be free to copy any materials except for those with copyright restrictions. Some files could be open to students, while other materials, such as quizzes or exams, would be restricted to teachers. Update each bank monthly, with each participating teacher taking a one-month term of responsibility for maintaining materials and overseeing additions to the collection.

| ACTIVITY 3.9 | Sharing Ideas and Teaching Tips |

Outcome

A sharing of new ideas, teaching tips, activities, and assessment strategies

Discussion and Procedure

Roundtable communities might be useful in order to share ideas and teaching tips that ensure quality lessons. Meet for lunch or after school once or twice a month to swap ideas and activities with a few other interested teachers. Give each participant an opportunity to share an activity that worked especially well. You can distribute the materials in a variety of ways: Make copies of each presentation for each teacher present.

Store the activities in a central bank after demonstrating your contribution. Invite a computer class to type the materials onto a disk or take turns transferring materials into a central computer program you can call Trading Teacher Materials. The librarian may permit you to use a filing cabinet so that students and teachers can remove materials on loan. The key is to present or discuss materials with other teachers over lunch or after school so that teachers know what activities are available and can enjoy collaborative illustrations.

ACTIVITY 3.10   Defining Evaluation Standards

Outcome
Teacher-identified assessment criteria for integrated projects

Discussion and Procedure
Before each new integrated unit, teachers meet to identify several key qualities that define an excellent project. After identifying some common assessment criteria, teachers collaborate with their students to finalize criteria lists. Assessment criteria are made available to all students, either on individual sheets or on large posters in each participating classroom. Following is a list of possible assessment criteria:

- relates to unit

- relates to life beyond the classroom

- displays knowledge, skills, and understanding

- exhibits student's strengths and abilities

- illustrates original work

- leads to further research on the topic

- is well organized

- makes good use of language

- integrates Gardner's eight ways of knowing

ACTIVITY 3.11   Overcoming Homework Obstacles

Outcome
A home study area where students can complete regular assignments and projects

Discussion and Procedure
Experts suggest that homework has a critical influence on academic achievement. In fact, some claim that consistent home study is the primary determinant of success in school. David Hargreaves of Cambridge University claims that regular homework is the equivalent of an extra year in the classroom. You can help par-

ents overcome their children's homework obstacles by teaching them how to create a regular homework area.

Have parents discuss with their sons or daughters the most suitable spot for doing homework. Homework areas should be easily accessible for students but out of the way of too much noise or family activity. Together, parents and children will prepare that area as a regular work area. It does not have to be elaborate; it can be a small desk in the bedroom or hall corner. Parents ensure that adequate lighting exists. They make a list of essentials and attempt to supply the highest priorities first. They will add supplies, such as writing materials, a dictionary, and ruler, as the needs arise. A small bulletin board or blackboard would serve as a message board as well as allow for a child's personal decorating touch.

ACTIVITY 3.12 Dialogue Journal for Parents, Students, and Teachers

Outcome
Weekly or biweekly communication among parents, students, and teachers

Discussion and Procedure
Communities allow moral codes to partner with psychological principles. Teachers, students, and parents are considered an integral part of decision making and are granted freedom to practice autonomy. Interactions can take many forms, such as dialogue journals.

Establish one or several dialogue journals in your classroom, with easy access for parents, students, and you. All journal entries should be dated and signed. Contributors may write paragraphs, lists, graphics, or sketches. Students can be creative. They can use vertical lines to separate lists, such as pros listed on one side of the page and cons listed on the other. Or they can use dialogue boxes, with areas for the writer's comments and for other people's responses. Several approaches and topics for journal entries may be used, including those that follow:

- enlisting parents' help for a project topic
- brainstorming new approaches to solving a problem
- sequencing one possible response to a problem
- exploring pros and cons of controversial issues
- raising questions about a discussion, reading, or project proposal
- communicating confusion about some aspect of the material being studied
- wondering about the feasibility of an experiment or hypothesis

- generating a progression of critical thinking exercises

- drafting an outline for a critical essay

- asking for help locating specific resources

THE POWER OF A STRESS-FREE MIND

Research shows that students do better in class when they use stress busters to help them. Once students catch hold of this fact, they tend to enjoy the learning process more.

Our three-pound brains continually rewire to learn better. But did you know your brain can also limit learning? Depression cuts creativity and blocks memory. Mood disturbances result in serotonin decline. As despair deepens, learning loss results.

Our brains are orchestrated by 200 kinds of cells with trillions of neural signals actively communicating in the cortex. As can be observed through brain imaging, brain chemicals seep through clefts in the brain and convert to electrical impulses, which impact what you learn and affect your reactions to life around you. Will you smile or sneer? Chemicals called neurotransmitters act as biochemical messengers that generate learning and act as stimuli to excite neurons or as inhibitors to suppress them. Drugs can stimulate or block synaptic transmission—another name for communication and electrical activity among neurons.

In spite of revelations, malfunctioning brains continue to hide keys that unlock problems and reveal learning patterns. We know that drugs such as Prozac block uptake of serotonin and hence depression. Unfortunately, some mind-altering drugs also affect mental abilities that help a person reflect, connect ideas, or think deeply. Physical exercise and good health increase oxygen and affect mood positively. Yet how or why this increases learning is less obvious.

We do know, though, that depressed people often lack images that comfort and console. Negative images and recriminating inner voices plague and disturb their thoughts. Imagine yourself failing at work today. Instead of inner mental responses that soothe and reassure you, depression shoots darts of fear and you dread further disasters. Although no cure exists for some forms of depression, hope and help have increased for many who face depression.

Determination alone is not enough to maintain well-being, since depression is ruled at times by our gene pools and at times by the lives we lead. Not surprisingly, brain researchers disagree on cures and causes for two common types of depression. One type, endogenous depression, originates from an innate predisposition to mood disturbances. Victims suffer despondency, hopelessness, or guilt over trivial triggers. Another kind, called neurotic or reactive depression, develops in response to external miseries like illness, death, or loss. Endogenous depression is often treated with mind-altering drugs or antidepressants. Reactive or neurotic depression is often treated with drugs in addition to psychological strategies that help people find more realistic views of their problems. Severe depression can be considered a psychotic condition. Even mild depression can generate personal misery.

We know that developing inner resources helps people refine images and stockpile positive emotional responses to combat mental difficulties. Everyone experiences fears and worries, and a failure of courage at times. But we can learn to face the future with hope. Reflection can aid us in creating a cache of positive images to block fear and deal realistically with negative events.

Build from Where You Are

In our global, increasingly technological society, people are living with new pressures. For some, this can result in bouts with depression. In 1990, President George Bush suggested that North America enhance public awareness of the benefits to be derived from brain research. Despite research breakthroughs, there is still no cure for depression. However, just learning more about how the brain works can help. For instance, when an alienated son learned that left-hemisphere damage tends toward depression while right-hemisphere damage can lead to manic behavior, he began to understand his parents more and to accept their differences. Leslie Hart (1983, p. 83) said it best in *Human Brain and Human Learning:* "With our new knowledge of the brain, we are just dimly beginning to realize that we can now understand humans, including ourselves, as never before, and that this is the greatest advance of the century, and quite possibly the most significant in all human history."

Brain-based tactics can benefit students who suffer depression. The brain itself is the most powerful force in any circle and can transform despair into learning. Faculty can help by allowing students to make mistakes and encouraging them to move beyond false starts. Einstein, who was ahead of his time in ways to work with our brains, understood that a person who never makes mistakes has never tried anything new. The key to growth here is to build on false starts without slipping into patterns of stress. Brain-based tactics can help sustain a calm mind and help us to think deeply or solve complex problems. Students need to be aware that stress can hinder learning. Knowing how to address stress can help students overcome the barriers that lead to stress and lead them to enhance their achievement.

Is It Possible to Avoid Stress?

Communication is stifled by stress, and so stress can make people feel isolated and alone. Stress also prevents our ability to grow and creates barriers to success. However, there is an answer. When stress hits us and our students, we can sidestep it by tapping into other parts of our brains. Teachers who learn to reduce stress in their own lives are more able to help students cope with their stressful situations.

Research on absenteeism and failure at work supports the fact that stress keeps both employers and workers from reaching their goals. But if we are alert to the signs of mental fatigue in ourselves and our students, we can often detect and prevent stress from spreading or causing harm. The following checklist can help in identifying stress:

Check the items that describe you:

- I find myself cussing at problems and people.   ———
- Others often get blamed for mistakes I make.   ———
- I put things off and avoid big decisions.   ———
- I tend to work longer and harder than normal.   ———
- Too often I avoid exercise and relaxation.   ———
- I eat too much junk food, even when I am not hungry.   ———

- I tend to avoid food and run my day on nervous energy.   _____

- My handwriting and other fine motor skills are poor lately.   _____

- I pad sentences with foggy words and rarely get to the point.   _____

- Rarely do I feel content and valued by others.   _____

- I take care of work and other people but avoid self-care.   _____

If your students' score on this survey is 5 or more, you will want to consider ways to address triggers that add stress. We can move past stress by employing a few easy-to-apply strategies. How do successful people cope with excessive stress? Rather than resigning themselves to live with stress, successful people find ways to exchange stress for more personal brainpower.

Strategies for Dealing with Stress

People who refuse to be crippled by stress tell us that they practice some or most of the following strategies to get beyond stress. Brain-based research also supports these practical tips:

1. **Discuss your annoyance with others.** Consult people you respect—friends, relatives, or counselors. Look for the source of frustration and listen to what others have to say about it. Ask questions about how others deal with similar problems. Listen to ways you can be good to yourself, and you will find you have more patience for others' shortcomings.

2. **Select a few battles to fight, and let the others slide.** Don't expend energy on every little thing. Instead, accept an error without condemning yourself. You will dance past your own mistakes with ease. The Wright Brothers achieved successful flights after many trial runs, showing that mistakes can be used as starting points for new discoveries.

3. **Set priorities.** Ask yourself what bite-sized pieces of work are critical to get done today, and put these at the top of your list. Add less important items under the essentials. Then add more trivial things last. Remember to be good to yourself. You will accomplish more and enjoy the process too! Successful people tell us that it is necessary to set priorities and not spread yourself too thin.

4. **Reorganize your time.** Build in some slack time for unexpected emergencies. Schedule regular time with family, friends and for leisure, just as you would plan for meetings and work events. You'll find if you stick to these times for restoration, as you would stick to other responsibilities, that stress flees.

5. **Budget daily stress triggers.** When we avoid clustering stressful situations and plan pleasant events in between more difficult ones, we give our brains an opportunity to bounce back in time for the next challenge.

6. **Exercise.** Bodily activity can produce a distinct relaxation effect and will prepare your brain for the stress you encounter. Did you know that your brain demands at least 20 percent of your total oxygen intake? That means that a healthy person exercises to maintain enough oxygen for body and mind. With exercise, we gain brain power to avoid stress and rise to challenges for positive results.

7. **Learn relaxation techniques.** Use deep breathing, imaging, biofeedback, or meditation. When we ignore our introspective intelligence, we decrease our ability to enjoy life. When we pause and reach deeper inside ourselves, we can often touch our spiritual center and enter into successful existence.

8. **Set aside some time for self-indulgence.** Our bodies tell us when we are overdoing it. When we learn to listen to our bodies, we act in positive ways that diminish stress and invite well-being. It is less a matter of what happens to us on any day and more a matter of how we respond to things that come into our day. We have all felt hardship strike us or others, and sometimes we can adopt a positive response that takes us to the other side of pain or anger.

9. **Move beyond yourself.** When we do something meaningful for someone else, it can give back goodness to us in unseen ways. One student suggested, "We can't out-give God," and it seemed to be true when the circle discussed this concept as it applied to their lives and their friends. Not that one gives to get back, but when people give something of themselves to others, they seem to generate more goodness to enjoy and pass around.

10. **Create consistent eating, sleeping, and exercise patterns.** Try eating heavier meals early in the day and lighter meals later. We gain more quiet rest and well-being when we exercise early in a day and then slow down gradually as evening approaches. We also sleep better with a quiet brain. Later in the book, I discuss practical ways to move active brain waves into quiet rest.

One teacher asked us "What does this have to do with my classes?" She explained, and rightly so, that teachers have enough to think about in just teaching secondary students. This is true. Nevertheless, since all students face stress at one point or another, and since brain experts tell us that stress reduces learning and diminishes students' chances for success in school, then stress is a factor to face in creating brain-based circles. It should also be noted that a certain amount of stress may actually be beneficial in motivating people to higher-quality performances. However, anxiety that comes from stress often robs creativity and prevents growth. We can bring these facts into our circles as practical tools for improvement.

We now know that human brains react to stress by producing hormones such as cortisol, which blocks learning or creating and prevents enjoyment of life. A person locked in stress misses the benefits of the day and emphasizes more problems than possibilities. This shows how stress prevents students from achieving and enjoying the best from learning experiences.

When students take care of stress through the strategies suggested here, they grow dendrite brain cells for higher achievement and success. They can develop habits for handling problems and letting parts of life roll off their backs.

More than ever before, we can now help ourselves, our students, and our colleagues to apply simple strategies to avoid undue stress or at least decrease its harmful effects. How people engage these strategies is proportionately linked to how well they develop and benefit from feelings of fulfillment and satisfaction. When they avoid or diminish stress, they find calm possibilities to solve the most difficult problems. This is why some students find success in difficult settings, while others succumb to rage, failure, or bitterness when pressures mount.

In roundtable communities, students take responsibility for solving their own problems through the identification and development of individual abilities within community. When one gift is valued to solve one aspect of a problem and another gift is valued to solve another aspect, students begin to risk using their own gifts and value more gifts from one another. A fireside chat climate can set the stage for these gifts to proliferate, which cannot happen in a lecture hall, where the teachers' gifts are the only ones presented.

In brain-based communities, where all intelligences are invited, developed, and welcomed, fewer specialists are required to stand and deliver traditional lectures and more students' gifts are engaged. One secondary teacher put it this way: "We reinvent the wheel with every student in our classes." Judging from the results he gets from most of his students, I can see why he would want students to own every new invention as they make their connections and to adapt the facts to their unique set of applications. In communities such as the one he created, parents and other volunteers integrate into the roundtables to share wisdom and learn alongside their sons and daughters. They dispel the myths that teens want to go it alone, and they have changed the culture so that parents feel welcome and respected as part of the learning process. Each participant is accountable to this learning community. Relationships are forged, cooperation increases, and more students' gifts are celebrated. As a result, they take away more.

CHAPTER 4

Building Roundtable Community through Integrated Projects

I must Create a System,
Or be enslav'd by another Man's.
I will not Reason and Compare,
My business is to Create.

William Blake

When we change the paradigm, we change the classroom atmosphere. For this reason, collaboration and communication about best practices should become a regular event in secondary and higher education circles. The opposite of brain-compatible progress and achievement growth is found in top-down, factorylike institutions. Whenever circles blossom into vibrant roundtable communities, we expect activities that represent this new paradigm, and that produce higher-quality results among students.

CREATING CLASSROOM COMMUNITIES

Teachers in my roundtables often ask, "What transforms an ordinary classroom into a caring community?" The following lists were gleaned from many discussions we have had on the distinguishing qualities of caring classroom communities.

Ten Identifying Factors of Classrooms as Community

1. inclusive language (or words that welcome all students and diminish none)
2. democratic decision making
3. active social intelligence
4. strong organization

5. involved members' interests and abilities

6. equal participation

7. listening skills

8. cooperative atmosphere

9. focused goals

10. pursuit of excellence

Ten Obstacles to Community Building in High Schools and Colleges

1. biased language

2. power imbalances

3. poorly developed social intelligence

4. poor organization

5. ignoring of members' interests and abilities

6. unbalanced participation

7. lack of listening skills

8. negative critiques

9. unfocused goals

10. lack of learning expectations

Ten Myths about Creative Classroom Communities

1. Language doesn't matter.

2. Nobody is in charge.

3. Classroom management suffers.

4. Teachers lack defined purpose.

5. Language skills diminish.

6. A few will dominate.

7. Students rarely learn to listen.

8. Quality learning is sacrificed.

9. Only a few really benefit.

10. Learning is haphazard.

The scenes and background knowledge described in this chapter are not meant for dispensing information to students. These are examples of scenes and knowledge that students, parents, and teachers in community can create. Through the integration of ideas and the contributions of many people's gifts, new ideas are created.

This chapter illustrates how brain-friendly communities differ from traditional learning settings. In brain-friendly circles, faculty and students find ways to rewire their brains daily for more success. They do this in part through understanding how brain waves impact learning opportunities and applying strategies to foster passion and purpose in class.

HOW BRAIN WAVES CAN HELP US TO PERFORM

Using brain-imaging technology, scientists can now watch a student's brain perform, and from this research has come facts about how brains work and how to rewire one's mind for better performance. The brain's activity is made up of waves that shift back and forth for different outcomes each day. Face an audience for the first time, for instance, and one type of brain-wave activity come into play. Then when you think deeply, in a quiet place, another type emerges. It's more complex than simply wanting to have active or quiet brain waves. Students can learn simple strategies to move from panic brain waves to sleep brain waves through engaging in a quiet moment or an inspired activity. An ideal goal for getting the most from brain-wave patterns is to strike a balance so that all waves operate at appropriate and equal times each day. The question is, how?

You can think of brain-wave activity as an escalator that moves you from active, excitable beta waves to reflective, quiet delta waves. If you've had a rough day, you might want a comfortable delta sleep, since deep thought and slumber both engage similar brain waves. We use brain waves to our advantage when we facilitate the waves appropriate to the results we want to get from any situation.

There is increasing interest in this topic. Perhaps this is because there are new evidences of brain waves at work in our lives. Or perhaps it is because there are more individuals who seem to have brain-wave malfunctions that result in low achievement. For these and other reasons, more people attempt to identify brain-wave patterns and find ways to work with these to improve their performance. The brain-wave patterns of successful people reflect a balance of faster and slower patterns so that there are adventures on one end and reflective insights at the other. Brain waves move progressively across this spectrum according to the mental activity engaged and to the brain's natural inclinations.

Our brain-wave activity is impressive. *Beta brain waves* kick in when we think logically, solve problems, and confront external stimuli. Beta waves often race and can bring panic at times. Being in beta runs the risk of thinking deeply about little and tiring yourself out about much. Imagine this wave as related to fast-paced or even panicky activity within your mind. Beta activity has its place, but you must slow down at times and reflect. *Alpha brain waves* provide images and visuals and an escape from reality. Too much alpha activity leads to excessive escapism and daydreaming. Too little makes you a human machine, without dreams that inspire. *Theta brain waves* engage the inner and intuitive subconscious. Theta waves trigger memories, sensations, and emotions. Sometimes we store secrets there, which we block out in times of pain to survive what we feel unprepared to encounter. *Delta brain waves* provide personal radar and feelings at the unconsciou level. In healthy doses, these signals create empathy, while too much delta activity can cause you to take on someone else's problems. If you feel you can read other people's minds, you probably have more delta activity than most. If you often find yourself in trouble for stepping on another's toes, you may engage less in delta activity.

Getting a picture of your students' brain-based activity can give you tools to help them move from one kind of wave activity to another. For example, wide-eyed with beta activity at midnight, people can coax their brains into quiet delta thought and then into delta places of sleep. New studies show how students can alter their brain-wave activity to speed up thought or slow it down in order to access deeper insights. Einstein used his brain waves to advantage to help him invent and find new pathways of thinking, and we can teach students to do the same.

Whether they feel adrenaline's push or enter into quieter zones, three exciting books can help faculty and students use their brain waves for higher performance.

Daniel Amen's book *Change Your Brain, Change Your Life* suggests ways to tackle anxiety, diminish anger, and break obsessions. Anna Wise's *The High Performance Mind* helps learners find practical tips for improved creativity, spirituality, and relationships. *A Symphony in the Brain* by journalist Jim Robbins explains some of the science behind tasks that can help train readers to activate brain frequencies not normally used.

These helpful books can pique your students' interest in brain breakthroughs and help them move forward in their achievement. These books offer you specific and practical steps you can use to select, create, and improve your brain-based circles. Students and faculty will enjoy any of these fascinating books.

ACTIVITY 4.1   Circle Talk

Outcome
Shared ideas about some aspect of the curriculum that will be applied effectively to improve an event today

Discussion and Procedure
This activity allows each student an opportunity to contribute and helps students to convert facts into tools for solving real-life problems. While students are permitted to not make comments, few remain silent. Even quiet students enjoy the uninterrupted time to voice their personal ideas as these relate to curriculum content.

Student Ideas about Resource management
~ survive
~ greedy
~ waste
~ responsibility
~ fish stocks
~ adults ruined
~ trees give life
~ streams + rivers
~ global help
~ cooperation
~ technology
~ communities
~ rebuilding

Teacher and students form a comfortable fireside-like circle for this activity, which helps students to relate what they know to improve how they live. Each student is passed the "talking stick" (which can be any meaningful or interesting object), at which time that student is encouraged to share an idea about the curriculum. Continue passing the talking stick around the circle. Only the student holding the stick may speak; others may not interact in any way except to listen. Teachers should also participate in this circle and should follow the same rules: to speak only when holding the talking stick. Students are not obliged to speak and may pass the stick on to the next person without comment, or they may simply ask a question. At the end of the activity, one or two students may wish to sum up, briefly repeating the ideas presented and showing the relevant applications to real-life problems.

ACTIVITY 4.2   Walking to Find a Metaphor

Outcome
An illustrated haiku poem using at least one metaphor from nature to relate natures' meaning found within art and applicable to improving understanding

Discussion and Procedure

On a nature walk, encourage students to listen to the sounds, feel textures, and observe colors and shapes. Some students may wish to carry tape recorders or sketch books. Exchange ideas about water as a life giver and see how lack of water shows in the brown or yellow tips of grass blades. Students can watch water sprinklers satisfy the thirst of parched grass. As students feel the warm rays from the sun, they might compare this sensation to their own emotional well-being. Ask the students to compare the scenes they encounter with happy feelings or sad feelings or disappointments.

Discuss with the students nature and its relationship with other aspects of their own lives. They should look for similarities and differences. Have them describe a personal experience in which they felt like a wilting blade of grass or that nourished and uplifted them like water-soaked blades of grass.

Have students look up the word *metaphor* in the dictionary. Have them each list four or five metaphors they encountered on the walk. Then have them illustrate and create a haiku about one of the metaphors. (Remember: a haiku must have three lines, with five syllables, seven syllables, and five syllables, respectively.) Students title and display their illustrated haikus.

ACTIVITY 4.3   Jigsaw for Problem Solving

Outcome

A roundtable solution to a problem related to the lesson

Discussion and Procedure

Begin the activity in home groups—that is, groups of four that you or your students choose randomly. Form a list of questions related to the main theme. Each group chooses one problem or question that will help them understand or explore some

aspect of that theme. Each home group chooses a different question from the list. Each person in the home group records the group's main ideas about the question. Give a different-colored strip of paper to each person in the home group, using the same assortment of colors for each home group. Students record their ideas on the colored paper and then join with the same colors for their "expert" group.

Each student shares home-group findings with his expert-group peers, using his notes for that question. Students discuss the connections and the new problems that arise, based on new knowledge provided. They write down input shared by each representative.

Students return to their home groups for a discussion based on the facts and ideas gathered. Each home group creates a visual or graphic poster to demonstrate its findings. Students share the posters with the entire class and then display them on the bulletin board. Students retain the sheets of facts and ideas as study guides for final tests or quizzes on the topic.

Example: World Hunger
Following are questions about world hunger that students generated using this process.

Home Group/Expert Group Questions

1. What are the major reasons for world hunger?

2. Who suffers from hunger in today's world?

3. Why have we not stopped world hunger?

4. Who is most responsible for world hunger?

5. Who in our society is helping most?

6. What are the major solutions to world hunger?

7. What can students do about the problem?

8. What past solutions are most helpful?

9. What past solutions are least helpful?

10. What problems do we face in addressing and responding to world hunger needs?

The key is to generate curiosity and then to direct students to the library, to your lecture notes as guides, to texts, to the Internet, and to other relevant places where they might find information. In roundtables, we reverse the order of questions so that students begin with the questions that will trigger them to find deeper and more relevant meanings from their facts. That differs from a text-based approach, which expects students to read the work first and answer fact-related questions at the end. Roundtables, like a good fireside chat, start at the end to motivate the beginnings. In brain-based circles, creative and productive insights follow when students actively engage in creating interesting expectations at the start.

ACTIVITY 4.4   Brainstorm for Group Project Activities

Outcome
A list of which of the eight ways of knowing each student might contribute to the final project

Discussion and Procedure
Have students brainstorm for one question their project will attempt to answer. They decide how many of Gardner's eight ways of knowing they can incorporate into their project, who is responsible for each intelligence, and how it will be used. Each person might be responsible for incorporating two of the intelligences into the entire presentation. Students go over the whole project to make sure they incorporate all eight ways of knowing into a well-organized presentation.

The idea here is that when they teach others as they learn themselves, students retain about 90 percent of their knowledge, compared to about 5 percent retention from lectures. Remind them that all sections of the presentation should be a response to the overall question and show them exact criteria expected from their research.

ACTIVITY 4.5   Fixing Humorous Bloopers

Outcome

Advertisements that make sense because they connect facts and figures to what people think, care about, and do

Discussion and Procedure

Students will discover how the brain works best when it connects new facts to something it already knows or experiences. They will make the related applications about how they can optimize their own brains in relating to any new facts they learn and apply.

The following are excerpts from classified sections of city newspapers. Have students rewrite the ads so they make sense.

- Auto Repair Service. Free pick-up and delivery. Try us once, you'll never go anywhere again.

- Our experienced Mom will care for your child. Fenced yard, meals, and smacks included.

- Dog for sale: eats anything and is fond of children.

- Man wanted to work in dynamite factory. Must be willing to travel.

- Stock up and save. Limit: one.

- Semi-annual after-Christmas sale.

- Three-year-old teacher needed for preschool. Experience preferred.

- Mixing bowl set designed to please a cook with round bottom for efficient beating.

- Girl wanted to assist magician in cutting-off-head illusion. Blue Cross and salary.

- Dinner special—Turkey $2.35; Chicken or beef $2.25; children $2.00.

- For sale: an antique desk suitable for lady with thick legs and large drawers.

- Now is your chance to have your ears pierced and get an extra pair to take home, too.

- We do not tear your clothing with machinery. We do it carefully by hand.

- For sale: three canaries of undermined sex.

- Great Dames for sale.

- Have several very old dresses from grandmother in beautiful condition.

- Tired of cleaning yourself? Let me do it.

- Vacation special: have your home exterminated.

- Swim in the lovely pool while you drink it all in.

- The hotel has bowling alleys, tennis courts, comfortable beds, and other athletic facilities.

- Get rid of aunts. Zap does the job in 24 hours.

- Toaster: a gift that every member of the family appreciates. Automatically burns toast.

- For rent: six-room hated apartment.

- Man, honest. Will take anything.

- Used cars: Why go elsewhere to be cheated? Come here first.

- Christmas-tag sale. Handmade gifts for the hard-to-find person.

- Wanted: hair cutter. Excellent growth potential.

- Wanted. Man to take care of cow that does not smoke or drink.

- Our bikinis are exciting. They are simply the tops.

- Wanted. Widower with school-age children requires person to assume general housekeeping duties. Must be capable of contributing to growth of family.

- And now, the superstore—unequaled in size, unmatched in variety, un-rivaled inconvenience.

- We will oil your sewing machine and adjust tension in your home for $1.00.

ACTIVITY 4.6   Suggestion Books

Outcome
A book in which students make suggestions for their classes and provide alterna-tive approaches, ask questions, or express gratitude for some aspect of the lesson

Discussion and Procedure
Keep one notebook for each class on the corner of a desk near the front of the room. Invite students to dialogue with one another and with you in the commu-nal journal. Students may make suggestions, ask questions, or pose alternatives. You can use the book to address issues of concern, or you can respond to indi-vidual comments.

INTEGRATED LEARNING:
A RESOURCES MANAGEMENT UNIT

How does your classroom rate? Strong communities are created by classrooms that become active circles of learners who take risks, depend on one another, and expect to succeed. These learning circles create a sense of *we* from the integra-tion of *I's.*

Let's say you have chosen to study natural resources management. Your unit integrates such diverse interests and issues as fishery management and logging practices and forest management. The unit also calls for integration of many ways of learning and reporting. Your students can use your lectures on a specific topic as a resource when you distribute them as hand-out sheets. They can also brainstorm in their circles to decide where the key facts are found. Along with your guidance and their peers' suggestions, they will decide how they can best access these facts and how to apply them as multiple intelligences solutions to the questions raised.

The question that most teachers ask is "If I do not lecture, and if I want students to dig deeper and find better answers, what will I do to make this happen?" While your approach will vary depending on time limits, students' capabilities, and your expectations for the work, students will be a wonderful resource to help define your approach, and they enjoy making suggestions about how to get the quality results expected for each task. It is most difficult for traditional teachers to make the initial shift from a stand-and-deliver method to active student engagement for deeper understanding in a roundtable climate. Once this shift is made, no teacher I have worked with has ever returned to the lecture format, where it is assumed that teacher talk equates to student learning.

Each lesson in this unit incorporates Gardner's eight ways of knowing. We have found that classes in which students do well and enjoy learning bring students on board first. Students might identify their previous knowledge about the topic and discuss skills and attitudes required for quality learning. Or they might brainstorm responses to the following questions:

- What do you think of as natural resources?

- Have these been managed well in your community? Explain.

- Who is most responsible for resource management?

- How is your life as a student influenced by resource management?

- Do you have opportunities for managing your community's resources?

- How would a fishery in your community fit into the world's natural resource management?

- Is there a better way to harvest fish?

- What field trips have you taken to explore your community's natural resources?

- How can computers help manage resources?

- Is wood wasted in your community? How?

- Without trees, what would your world be like?

- What do you think about global warming?

- If you had to write an essay introducing your audience to world forestry, what would your title be?

- What indicators show a stream's deterioration? Can you think of a cure?

The key is to first hook the students. In other words, to hook new knowledge onto something they already know about a topic. What do they care about this topic? Or what don't they care about?

Applying the Multiple Intelligences Approach

After students have brainstormed possible responses to such questions, you and your students can consider possible group or individual expressions that accord with the multiple intelligences approach, as follows:

Verbal-linguistic

- Write a letter to your newspaper editor suggesting a solution to one current natural resources management problem in your community.

- Write a speech for a community leader to deliver on TV.

- Interview a well-known conservation expert on a mock radio program.

- Write a poem, play, or essay or produce a brochure to show some aspect of resource management.

Mathematical-logical

- Graph a tree- or other plant-replacement program in your area.

- Report statistics on the resource management programs in your community; show how the statistics can be interpreted.

- Prepare a cost analysis statement of a good resource management educational program for the public.

- Present a statistical report that would encourage more interest in conservation. How can big business help?

Musical-rhythmic

- Prepare a musical play for the class involving some aspect of resource management. Express your story, mood, and setting through carefully selected or created music.

- Use humor, tragedy, history, or biographical material put to music in order to tell your story.

- Write a song that expresses your ideas about the problems and solutions.

- Choose background music that reflects the problem; then present music that reflects an ideal solution.

Visual-spatial

- Draw a blueprint for a center to educate the public on resource management.

- Create posters for teaching and expressing the key issues.

- Create a school newspaper, with cartoons and diagrams, to increase awareness among your peers about one major controversy. Use art or graphs to show various perspectives of the issue.

- Present a slide show or create a photo album to show problems and solutions.

Bodily-kinesthetic

- Videotape the neighborhood resources and use your tape to create a classroom discussion. You might include scenes from family activities or from created role-plays.

- Organize a dance to express your ideas about natural resources and their future management in your community.

- Organize a mock rally and show how you would make a difference.

Interpersonal

- As a radio talk show host, interview four experts on resource management and get their opinions of best solutions.

- Interview members of your class for their ideas about the problems and solutions.

- Prepare a debate with others in your group and present this debate to the class.

Intrapersonal

- Write an essay for a local magazine about who owns the problems and what should be done to manage our resources.

- Pretend you are a logger, an antilogger, a Greenpeace leader, and a fisher. Keep a diary as each person for one week.

- Observe your school's resource management and chart your observations. What is your opinion of the school's management? What improvements do you suggest?

Naturalistic

- Compare problems and possibilities in a natural disaster.

- Interview a naturalist about the problem and solutions.

- Create a natural museum or display to organize and exhibit your findings.

Purpose of the Unit

The purpose of this unit is not only to learn new material, but also to reflect on impressions, to create new understanding, and to hear the ideas of many others. New ideas on resource management will emerge from news articles, textbooks, experts, peers, personal reflections, and so on. The idea of the unit is to consider more than one perspective on all key issues and to apply knowledge to new situations and challenges in the community. While learning significant facts about resource management is important, more important is the application of those facts to real-life situations in the community.

Sample Project: Forest Management

Background Information

The forest industry benefits from new technology. Forestry companies use aerial and digital maps to plan their harvests. Satellites provide foresters with information. Forest fires are monitored and controlled by radar. Damage is controlled by sprays and biological discoveries. Not all technology has helped forestry to progress, however. Sprays and biological pest control (bringing in one species to consume another) can harm fish- and bird-feeding patterns. Use of this technology can also change the breeding patterns of harmful insects, so dangerous insects actually increase. While researchers can control some insects using these methods, biological pest technology is usually expensive and slower than spraying.

Logging Practices: The Debate

You might use a debate to investigate both sides of the logging issue. The following statement might result from student discussion and form the basis of the debate: *We have to clear-cut the steep side hill country. There is no other viable way to get good timber to the roadside.*

Side 1 argues for the statement and shows that, while clear-cutting will have some negative impacts on the environment, there are more important issues, such as a family's income. Side 2 opposes the statement and shows that, although some people may lose their jobs, the larger issue is that clear-cutting is contributing to the destruction of our planet.

You would encourage students to research the claims they make. At the beginning of each debate, write the debate statement on the board. Underneath, list the names of people on side 1 and the names of people on side 2. Beside the names, write *pro* or *con* so that the audience and judges can follow the arguments.

Following the debate, the audience asks questions and makes comments. Three students, chosen in advance, are the judges. They vote anonymously, then make comments to each team. Following is a list of statements to guide the judges in offering effective comments to each side.

Defending Position

1. You provided this strong data and defended these points well: . . .

2. You showed strong arguments when . . .

3. You predicted objections when . . . and responded by . . .

4. You spoke well, articulated well, and engaged the audience through eye contact and . . .

Rebuttal

1. You addressed opponents' concerns when . . .

2. You showed respect for opponents when . . . but opposed their points effectively when . . .

3. You predicted the opposition when . . . and actually convinced the audience otherwise when . . .

4. You addressed comments for the audience well when . . .

Select three student judges to constructively critique the teams. They may choose to go over the statements and add such phrases as *did not.* Then they offer some suggestions for what each side might have argued instead or show how the sides could have used data to strengthen arguments. Don't worry if the students miss details. Others will also be commenting. But students should aim for at least one positive suggestion and one constructive suggestion for each side. It would be even better to have one positive comment and one constructive suggestion for both defenses and rebuttals.

Once students have judged a few debates, they will rely less on written guidelines and more on their own informed insights. But in the beginning, you may find the above guidelines useful, and so may your students.

Logging Practices: Role-Play

Another option would be to have students develop the following scenarios and role-play them or simply read and discuss them in groups.

Scenario 1

Jim pleads with a major logging company to stop clear-cutting in a forest with ancient trees. He writes letters, signs petitions, sets up blockades, and threatens to stop the workers forcefully. Nobody appears to hear Jim's concerns. When a concerned neighbor tells Jim he should consider tree spiking as a final resort, Jim wonders if this approach might be the only way to get loggers to stop logging and listen. Jim's girlfriend, Sue, is against tree spiking because of the injuries it causes. They go for coffee to discuss their next move.

Students might develop the following questions from this role-play:

- What are some possible reasons the loggers do not listen to Jim?
- How should Jim make his concerns known?
- Should Jim use tree spiking to try to stop the logging?
- Will Sue influence Jim? How?
- After hearing both arguments, which one do you agree with?

Scenario 2

You have been a logger for your entire adult life. Logging is the only way you know how to earn a living to support your five children. Environmentalists have moved into your area in order to protest logging as a menace to the environment surrounding your community. Local journalists arrive at your door to ask you for an interview. They want solutions and ask you to make a statement for the front page of their paper. You say . . .

Students might develop the following questions from this role-play:

- Why have the environmentalists come, in your opinion?
- How should you respond to the protests?
- Should you stop logging? What are your alternatives?
- Will protesters influence you? How?

Scenario 3

Five students decide to take logging matters into their own hands. They are tired of the environmentalists' actions that cause workers to lose pay and make their friends and family members feel guilty for going to work. They are also tired of the workers cutting down trees in ways that may harm the environment. They are concerned that their children will not know what it is like to have a forest so close. The students plan an evening to resolve the problem. They cancel their regular Thursday volleyball night to discuss the issues; their enthusiasm for this cause has risen. Their meeting turns out to be a huge success. Other people seem interested in the issues and are willing to join and look for answers together. The students present their solutions to the town council the following week. The solutions accepted at the meeting are . . .

Students might develop the following questions from this role-play:

- What do the environmentalists want?

- What do the loggers want?

- What compromises might each side be willing to make?

- Why do students care about the outcomes?

- After hearing both arguments, how can you integrate both sides' ideas to find a compromise?

Scenario 4

You are an environmentalist, and you have many facts that show how the logging practices in your community harm the environment. Your favorite brother is a logger and a hard worker who believes that logging is a good job. He wants to invest his future in the community's logging company. Your discussions with your brother become bitter when environmentalists set up protest lines and your brother cannot work. You decide you could make a difference, and so after discussions with several community leaders, you decide to . . .

Students might develop the following questions from this role-play:

- What do the environmentalists have against your brother's work?

- What does your brother want from you?

- What alternative actions might each side be willing to take to find a solution?

- What do your other family members think about the problem?

- After discussions with all family members, what compromise can you suggest?

Scenario 5

Your girlfriend sits in on a meeting of loggers and, after listening to several moving speeches, felt very badly for families who might lose their houses because logging jobs are no longer guaranteed in their community. You know many of these families and you know their children. But after hearing your girlfriend's arguments for logging, you remain convinced that environmentalists are right and logging is bad for the community. Your girlfriend threatens to break off your relationship, which you care deeply about, if you do not change your position. You decide . . .

Students might develop the following questions from this role-play:

- What does your girlfriend really want?

- Why has your girlfriend chosen this side of the issue?

- What compromises might your girlfriend be willing to make?

- Can you change her decision to end your relationship?

- After hearing both arguments, how can you integrate both sides' ideas to find a compromise?

Sample Project: Harvesting Fish

In this project, students might research a fish farm. They could describe it and show how it operates. Following are questions they could consider:

- Who owns the farm?

- Who works at the operation?

- What do the jobs require?

- How do fish farms help overfished communities?

- Are there disadvantages to these farms?

- How important is the fish farm to the fishing industry?

- What are advantages and disadvantages of fish farming compared to open-sea fishing?

- What conditions ensure the success of a fish farm?

- How can fish farmers overcome obstacles to the fish-farming industry?

Background Information

Progress in fishing technology has changed the way fishers work. Many fish species are dwindling. New technologies, such as sonar, have increased fishers' ability to find and catch fish. As a result, many countries have set fishing quotas. These quotas have resulted in fishers' searching for new ways to harvest fish. Many raise fish in confined environments. Aquaculture, or fish farming, uses genetic research. Researchers have also developed new, cost-effective fish foods made from plant proteins.

Project Format

Just as with the logging project, students might hold a debate that addresses the pros and cons of fish farms. Or they might present reports and discuss the implications of fish farming for workers, owners, the government, the community, and so on. Or they might role-play leaders of a community who want to do the best for all its members and make recommendations about fish farming in the future.

FARMING UNIT

Technology has created new uses and new demands for farm products. The focus of this unit would be on the influence of new farming technology on communities.

Background Information

One hundred and fifty years ago, farming methods used in North America were similar to those used in medieval Europe. Gradually, however, human effort and horsepower were replaced, first by steam-powered machines and then by gasoline-powered machines. Now, farming in North America is almost completely mechanized. In 1930, a North American farmer might have had ten workers, fifteen horses, a steam- or gasoline-powered tractor, and a threshing machine. By 1990, a farmer could harvest the same number of crops in less time by using a combine that cuts, separates, and cleans grain in a single operation. This farmer also would use chemicals to control insects and weeds.

Genetic engineering has also affected farming. Plants grown for food have been genetically altered to resist diseases, grow faster, and produce more. Genetic engineering has also resulted in cows that produce more milk and pigs that have less fat.

Some people are concerned that many of these new technologies may upset the ecosystem. Gasoline-powered machines pollute the air. Genetic engineering narrows the diversity of plant species so that they are susceptible to diseases that attack through one characteristic. Chemicals seep into water supplies and kill animals, fish, and plants.

Activities and Assessment Strategies

To be fair to all students, assessment should not be restricted to paper-and-pencil tests. It should consider a variety of projects. Assessment of students' success in this farming practices unit might include one or several of the activities that follow:

1. **Visual-spatial:** Students might research the farming industry and show the ways in which technology has influenced it. To illustrate the changes in farming that have taken place over the last sixty-five years, students create models of a farm that uses human and horse power and one that uses modern technology. They may use art, symbols, a collage, or photography in the project. The work should reflect what they learned through their research.

2. **Mathematical-logical:** Students use numbers to represent the changes in farming that have taken place over the past sixty-five years. They show costs, family budgets, and income expectations, and compare these figures. They might calculate the number of successful U.S. farms in 1930 and the number of successful U.S. farms that exist today.

3. **Verbal-linguistic:** Students might write a research report or a two-act play in which they compare the farming methods used in 1930 to those used in 1990. They could show how farming has influenced their community and how community life has influenced and changed farming.

4. **Musical-rhythmic:** Students write a song about farming, showing their reactions to the methods used in 1930 and to the technologies used today. Students could research what kind of music farmers played in their communities or how music has changed on an average farm from the early 1990s to now.

5. **Bodily-kinesthetic:** Using cardboard, blocks, or other materials, students re-create a farm from the early 1900s or a farm in the 1990s. The mock-up should show what farm life was like in that era.

6. **Interpersonal:** Each student interviews someone who has been farming for at least thirty years. Students ask about the ways in which farming has changed during this time.

7. **Intrapersonal:** A student writes two journal entries, one as a farmer in 1900 and the other as a farmer in 1990.

8. **Naturalistic:** Students collect data from farms to describe results and photograph natural patterns and shapes of farming equipment to describe results over time.

OTHER TOPICS FOR INTEGRATED UNITS

You might also do a unit on mining and have students research how various minerals became important during specific stages of North American development. For example, many new minerals now being mined, such as uranium and cadmium, became important only after technology created uses for them. Or students could investigate advances in mining exploration during the 1940s and how this expanded the mining industry.

Following are more possibilities students might investigate:

1. How does heavy-duty equipment bring ore to the surface?

2. Once minerals are located, how do scientists test the worth of the deposits?

3. Compare strip mines and underground mines.

4. Explain how draglines clear away top layers of soil to expose minerals.

5. Why are strip mines safer than underground mines, and for whom?

6. Describe the oil sands in the Athabasca.

7. Describe the oil sands on the Persian Gulf.

8. In what ways did technology change coal mining?

ACTIVITY 4.7 | Profile Your Students' Strengths

Outcome
A thumbnail sketch of your students' greatest skills in the eight intelligences

Discussion and Procedure
This activity will indicate where most of your students' strengths or weaknesses exist. This profile may help you and your students plan a variety of activities that activate all eight ways of knowing any lesson. Your profile might look like the chart in Figure 4.1.

Pass out two index cards to each students. On one card, students complete the statement "My highest interest is . . . " in one word. On the second card, students complete the statement "My highest ability is . . . " in one word. Under each of the eight ways of knowing listed on the bulletin board, place the students' cards so that the edge of one card touches the edge of the one next to it. Tape the cards in place to form a graph of students' interests and abilities. Interests and abilities will be mixed in the class profile. You could participate in this activity by adding your own cards. You do not need to include names. You may wish to record these responses somewhere and then repeat a similar profile several months after classroom activities in all eight ways of knowing.

You might vary this activity by profiling students' expressed weaknesses to create more activities that would allow students to develop weaker areas.

FIGURE 4.1   Sample Student Profile Using Gardner's Eight Ways of Knowing the World

Mathematical-logical	Plays chess Organizes Solves problems	*Interpersonal*	Helps friends Listens and acts for others Advises Cares
Verbal-linguistic	Debates Writes poetry Writes stories Speaks	*Intrapersonal*	Thinks and records in journal Does yoga Imagines life through other's view Admits strengths and weaknesses
Visual-spatial	Creates works of art Paints Draws	*Naturalistic*	Spends time in natural settings Collects data from nature Demonstrates solutions from nature
Musical-rhythmic	Plays drums Sings Creates background music		
Bodily-kinesthetic	Plays sports Builds Acts in drama Builds computer program		

ACTIVITY 4.8   Activate Your Family's Intelligences

Outcome
A chart designed to log the progress of students' family members in developing their own intelligences

Discussion and Procedure
Students can complete the following activities over a period of time. List each event on a card and allow students to check off the completed activities. Groups of students who complete similar activities compare results and discuss the difficulties. In groups during class, students create a list of questions to ask family members. Invite parents into the classroom to discuss the project with the class. Have students create posters that describe their families. They should also write thank-you notes to each member of their families. The notes should celebrate the stated interests and strengths of that family member. Students might also create a family tree or a collage that shows the interests and abilities of family members for a classroom display of students' intelligence roots.

1. **Logical-mathematical:** Students survey favorite activities and highest abilities of family members. They list family's abilities and interests on a chart. Which members do they most resemble? Least resemble?

2. **Verbal-linguistic:** At the dinner table, students discuss racism and show how their own opinions of others have been shaped and how they have changed over time. They identify the problems in their community and suggest ways of improving our appreciation of different cultures.

3. **Musical-rhythmic:** Students stroll through a park with their families after dinner. They listen to the sounds of nature. When they return home, they play

music that best reflects the experience. They identify other music that reflects their friendships, their down days, or their frustrations at school.

4. **Visual-spatial:** Students invite family members to draw cartoons of their day. They discuss ways to improve tomorrow or to maintain the success they experienced today.

5. **Bodily-kinesthetic:** With other family members, students run through a field, play tennis, or dance. They feel their bodies moving quickly and think about what messages their brains are sending to their muscles while they exercise. They discuss some different ways they can learn a new skill when the body is in motion.

6. **Interpersonal:** Students and families brainstorm activities that involve relating to others, mutual respect, multicultural understanding, group problem solving, and so on.

7. **Intrapersonal:** Students interview each family member to find out what each person likes and dislikes and why. They brainstorm for solutions to dislikes and reasons for likes. They record their responses.

8. **Naturalistic:** Students walk outside in search of a natural icon that best describes their abilities or illustrates the vision of their team.

ACTIVITY 4.9   Explore Your Students' Interests

Outcome
An inventory that reflects on and reports what each student knows or cares about

Discussion and Procedure
Students respond to the following to express their interests and relate any prior knowledge about a topic.

- Three words that describe me are . . .
- Things I like to do when I'm not in school are . . .
- I would like to learn more about . . .
- Someday I would like to . . .
- Learning is fun when . . .
- If I could have anything I wanted at school, it would be . . .
- I like to be praised for . . .
- When I've done something well at school, I like to be acknowledged by . . .
- I wonder a lot about . . .
- I like people who . . .
- Sometimes I worry about . . .
- One thing that really bothers me is . . .
- Something that really challenges me is . . .
- One thing I know about myself is . . .

(This inventory was developed by Campbell, Campbell, and Dickinson [1992, p. 143].)

To vary this activity, alter the questions to invite students to state what they know about the topic being introduced and what they hope to find out. This works especially well as a classroom management technique, where students seem disengaged, because it allows students to start where they are and to move forward in ways that combine their strengths. The emphasis is on the fact that although students learn differently, no one style is preeminent. People simply learn best in different ways. Some people call this variation *learning styles,* a term that emerged in the 1970s as teachers attempted to describe diverse approaches to problem solving, meeting common standards in uniquely different ways, and communicating results.

LEARNING STYLES AND MULTIPLE INTELLIGENCES

While the backbone of MI is that each person comes to class with at least eight distinctive intelligences, learning styles enable students to blend and combine these intelligences in several recognized patterns. Learning styles relate to the learning approaches that students enjoy most, as follows:

• **Visual:** Enjoys concepts, pictures, and charts. While others may have difficulty with graphics, visual learners enjoy bringing ideas to life through colors, lines, or constructions.

• **Kinesthetic:** Enjoys high levels of activity and movement. Learning often comes more naturally, through physical movement.

• **Analytic:** Enjoys looking at the bigger picture and breaking ideas up into manageable parts. Likes to create order out of chaos and can always find a good starting point.

• **Global:** Enjoys shaping an overall concept and translating ideas into terms that others can understand. Fits similar pieces into a bigger picture.

• **Concrete sequential:** Enjoys organization and detail and can usually chart time well for creating projects. Likes to transform abstract ideas and concepts into concrete realities.

• **Abstract sequential:** Enjoys checking and documenting information. Takes time and effort to research and evaluate information to ensure accuracy, value, and credibility.

• **Concrete random:** Enjoys creating interesting adventures. Enjoys inspiring, motivating, and energizing others, pushing a group toward new adventures.

Along with other approaches described in this book, learning styles can be adapted into classroom management techniques and can help teachers to work with special needs students. In order to help students to identify their learning style preferences, and to adapt these to work well in your classes, you can start with one problem they are having. For instance, common problems tend to include

• organization of ideas or materials

• inability to work well with others

- boredom with the material

- lack of reflection required to improve their work

Once students have identified a problem area or you have seen a growth area, ask questions that will help students to select a strategy that they enjoy most to attain the results you expect. As they list the strategies together, they are likely also illustrating their preferred learning styles. Students are especially good at helping one another with this practice. That's why this can act as a classroom management technique: it gets students involved through activating their preferred approaches to the work.

In the roundtable learning approach, students first work together with a teacher's guidance to create a safe learning setting. Lecture handouts are often distributed to students as learning tools, and Web resources as well as texts and current course materials are made available. Students are taught to take leadership in the areas of their strengths and to both teach and learn from every member of the group so that teams prosper and students benefit.

Learning styles are especially useful in classes when teachers provide clear guidelines, make suggestions for alternative approaches, and encourage creativity within structure. It's good to remember that high school students sometimes have had very little experience relating to peers in their classes. Others have been put into groups without clear guidance or motivation and so have suffered negative results. Roundtables cultivate most of the learning styles when they challenge all students to take risks, create expectations that students can attain, and value or reward superior quality for its own sake. Faculty motivate students most by showing keen interest in all they care about and by encouraging them to improve almost everything they do. This is how their brains work best.

HEALTH AND LEARNING

In spite of all one does to help some students, barriers to behavior and to learning seem inevitable. You'll also want to pay attention to their health. There are medical reasons why some young people are getting less than they should from their brains. When faculty understand the signs to watch for, they can begin to help some students overcome the most stubborn barriers. Solutions are not easy, but research has been offering more alternatives in the past few years.

One woman at my Learning Renewal Center told me, "Two of my five children are hyperactive, and teachers suggest they should be tested and placed on drugs. If I do not want meds to rob their creativity and enthusiasm, what can I do to help them to settle down and concentrate in school?" Teens who are diagnosed with attention disorders such as ADHD (attention deficit hyperactivity disorder) are often given Ritalin or Adderall. While the trend toward treatment with drugs is on the rise, and while teens have a hard time coping with these disorders, doctors are offering alternatives. You may wish to check with school specialists to learn more about restrictive diets, vitamin and mineral supplements, brain-wave-measuring technology, or biofeedback and other useful aids.

No single test for these conditions works for all individuals, and doctors don't always agree on the diagnosis, but it helps to be aware of the research. We are told that Ritalin is a powerful stimulant that calms ADHD teens and improves mental focus. We also know that similar results can come from alternative approaches.

In spite of the fact that nontraditional therapies remain largely untested, re-searchers have begun to evaluate alternative therapies in a scientifically rigorous way.

David Rabiner, a researcher at Duke University, operates a Website (http://www.helpforadd.com) that tracks studies of several alternative treatments that hold promise and are put to rigorous tests. Following are some alternatives that have been studied:

1. **Diet.** The notion that food dyes, preservatives, and other ingredients can cause mental problems has been explored. Researchers at the University of Alberta in Calgary found that elimination of certain foods improved behavior in 12 of 24 hyperactive preschool-age boys. German researchers also found that 12 of 49 school-age children with ADHD showed similar improvements when on similarly restricted diets. It is important to get support from a doctor or health specialist to treat attention problems with food elimination methods. It is also important to chart and record progress.

2. **Supplementation.** Studies have pointed out that teens might benefit from vitamin or mineral supplements, but there are cautions to this alternative approach also. For instance, vitamin A, zinc, and iron can all be toxic in high dosages. It's always best to gain support of a medical specialist you trust in order to decide what doses and what supplements are needed to improve attention.

3. **Biofeedback.** This practice helps teens train themselves to focus more deeply and continuously by controlling the electrical activity in their own brains. Using EEG technology, experts can help teens with ADHD increase their abnormally lower-frequency brain-wave patterns, those patterns found in the frontal cortexes of people diagnosed with these disorders. Teens are taught to concentrate on patterns and mazes while they receive "neurofeedback" signals from an EEG. Using this technology, teens can consciously alter their brain-wave activity to create better focus. The problem for teens and teachers is that there are no accepted standards or guidelines by which to evaluate the effectiveness of biofeedback treatments. So each doctor, psychologist, or therapist has his or her own methods and machines. Some have teens solve puzzles or try to recognize patterns while tracking brain waves; others have them concentrate on a certain point on a video screen while attempting to focus; still others are marketing video machines for in-home use. Also, biofeedback therapy can cost from $50 to $100 a session, and specialists recommend two or three sessions a week, for about fifty sessions in all. This cost and time commitment is not appropriate for all families, schools, or teens, but there are other methods to start.

4. **Behavioral therapy.** Marsha, a fifteen-year-old secondary student, unable to concentrate for more than a few minutes at a time, was diagnosed with ADHD as a high school freshman. She refused to go on medication because she was an artist and was afraid her creativity would suffer if she was drugged daily. With support from her parents, Marsha set daily targets, and this small step gave her surprising success at home and at school. At home she posted lists and bulletin boards; at school she kept a detailed calendar and a strict set of deadlines. She rewarded herself when she kept these daily targets, and her parents added extra allowance and TV privileges. Marsha and her parents successfully engineered a working program of behavioral therapy, and they communicated progress regularly to her teachers. The results amazed everybody! Research backs the fact that, with intensive use of target setting, organizational tactics, and time management

skills, 30 to 50 percent of teens with attention problems can be helped to increase their motivation and achievement at school and in the home.

There are wonderful new tips coming out daily about how to get more from our brains in school. Unfortunately, many of these innovative ideas are not getting into our teens' classes. This is not to blame any person or system. When classes work well, they help teens to use their brains well. Teachers can do a great deal to help teens. By making learning fun, for instance, you'll get farther. Go with your gut! Don't take action if you sense a 40 percent chance of being right, but don't wait until you are a 100 percent sure. By then it is almost always too late. What would it take for you and your students to risk going with your gut in a class today?

You can train bright, willing students in the fundamentals of any lesson, but brain-based roundtables stir up in all learners the integrity, judgment, energy, balance, and the drive to apply real solutions to complex problems.

CHAPTER 5

The Roundtable Approach to Creative Risk Taking

One way to encourage people to take creative risks is to reward them for it.

Tom Melohn

From childhood we learn to avoid mistakes. Risk takers make many mistakes. Thinking independently is risky. So we learn to avoid independent thought. Creativity causes something within us to connect to something outside of us, but creativity also requires risk. How can we overcome the fear of taking risks in order to connect inner creativity to life?

We benefit from risk taking whenever we view our mistakes as stepping stones to creativity rather than as obstacles. Ralph Waldo Emerson said, "In every work of genius we recognize our own rejected thoughts." Roundtable learning helps us overcome the fear of making mistakes. It reaches beyond facts to make contact with the elusive muse of insight. Creative risk taking exposes our understanding of a topic. Even if members of a roundtable show "fuzzy" understandings, side stepping, or vague notions of an undeveloped picture, they are encouraged.

The fact is, we all meet with failure, but a creative risk taker learns how to move beyond mistakes and failures. In 1836, Abraham Lincoln's business failed, yet he made other business ventures. In that same year, he lost his bid for renomination to run for Congress, yet he took a risk and sought nomination to run for president in 1854. He was not nominated. Also, he lost his senate race in 1858. Mistakes for Lincoln, however, translated into courage and compassion, because he turned his attention to converting errors into educational opportunities. His mistakes created entrance points into new ideas.

Why do we push students and teachers to hide their mistakes and avoid risks? Why not accept mistakes as part of being human? Like the skin horse in Margery Williams's *The Velveteen Rabbit,* we enjoy learning more when masks and pretense are absent. Creative people such as Albert Einstein enjoy a wide variety of experiences, take risks, and admit mistakes. "A person who never makes a mistake never tried anything new," Einstein said.

ADOPTING NEW ATTITUDES ABOUT MISTAKES

We can develop new ways, new attitudes, and new techniques to approach mistakes. We can learn new ways from past mistakes when we adopt new attitudes and attempt new techniques. Our memories of mistakes challenge us to do so.

Unfortunately, some teachers respond to our mistakes and failures with negative reactions. One grade 10 student described how a teacher snapped at her, "That was a stupid answer!" Another high school student refused to volunteer answers after being humiliated in a math class. Students put down for errors will avoid taking risks. If we treat errors as wrong ideas or risks as bad choices, we will mark students' efforts with a red *X*. Mistakes are personal blunders and often a natural consequence of creative risk taking. Risks are not encouraged in classrooms where only water-tight answers are rewarded with high grades or where ambiguity is not tolerated. Students' comments tell it better:

> All my teachers knew I had messy handwriting, and this would probably extend itself to drawing too. Had the teacher thought about how difficult it was for me to draw the relevant details of the bacteria we observed through the microscope, she might not have laughed at my diagram. I felt like I had failed the task. To this day I still hate drawing because of my embarrassment over that science class.

> My art teacher insisted we splash every kind of color and texture on our papers. I was especially skilled at drawing realistic and real-life images, and so I got a low B in my best subject.

My personal insights about converting errors into opportunities are a culmination of experiences gained through twenty years of teaching high school and lecturing at universities. My experience suggests that high schools let too many of us down. In the MITA model, we view mistakes as creative stepping stones toward more integrated understandings. We have fewer paper-and-pencil tests and more questions posed by students as they make judgments, integrate criticism, and reconsider problems while investigating real possibilities.

If we recognize the individuality of every learner, we must also accept the need for a curriculum tailored to each individual—a curriculum that describes progress by using more than a single ruler. Outcome-based education, constructivist education, and community-based education, for example, may help students benefit from their risk taking and to learn from mistakes.

OUTCOME-BASED LEARNING APPROACHES

Over the last forty years, a new approach to learning, outcome-based education (OBE), has evolved. Researchers Spady and Marshall (1991) highlight OBE's three central premises that influence learning.

- All children can learn and succeed, although not in the same way or on the same day.
- Success breeds success and is therefore required by all students to meet their goals.
- Schools usually determine the conditions of success and can alter those conditions.

In OBE, all aspects of the curriculum are centered on the specific goals that students must reach by the end of the unit. OBE practices provide useful ways to build new neuron pathways from what a student knows at any given moment to what students are expected to know by the end of a lesson or assignment. For this reason, each person in the brain-based circle is aware of each curriculum goal

expected. In MITA roundtable learning, this clear focus usually begins with a question such as *How do you write a business letter using persuasive speech?* Many ideas are brainstormed, and no one idea is preferred over the others initially. While students' responses will differ, nevertheless the highest learning priorities in these circles are concise and compelling, not cluttered and confusing. Brain-based targets convey a clarity of purpose, credibility of direction, and carefully planned organization.

When organization includes integration, as it does in most fireside-chat circles, learners grow accustomed to sorting out facts in a wider variety of ways to accommodate this integration. In other words, while targets simplify and clarify, they also relate to reality so that students can make regular applications. This book's organization is one example of that integration in that it is organized more for application than for memorization of lists.

Integration of facts enables students in any circle to respond with their own questions, celebrate differences among their peers, and find further solutions to problems within cultural diversity. At the same time, students are encouraged to test the brain facts provided in order to explore how these new facts from neuroscience can improve their tools for learning success. Even though the jury is still out on some of the brain insights provided here, participants benefit because they hear a wide variety of ideas to investigate in their own lives and because their diversity is respected as they progress. Roundtable communities maximize the use of all resources by optimizing each person's unique contributions so that every participant will benefit.

In outcome-based learning, specific goals generate an activity, product, or performance that can be measured. Students and teachers sometimes collaborate to define the criteria. They brainstorm a list of common standards by which the final product will be evaluated. Outcome-based learning activities meld with roundtable learning to help students take creative risks and plan their own units. In this way, students take ownership for their evaluation, understand their achievement targets, and enjoy opportunities to apply their ideas in a real-life setting.

ACTIVITY 5.1   Creating Checklists to Guide Work

Outcome
Student-created checklists that guide their work and provide an assessment tool for editing and completing final copy

Discussion and Procedure
Students can create these checklists in large groups, with the entire class, or in smaller groups. They should submit the checklists with the project so you can assess how each student uses checklists.

Students brainstorm a relevant checklist that will guide a quality project on the chosen topic. They refer to the checklist while doing the project and at the end of the project. They respond to the checklist, answering any relevant questions and providing brief explanations for questions that did not relate to the final work. They attach the checklists and their responses to the projects as part of the assessment tool. They add any new questions to their checklists that they consider relevant as they work on the project. Finally, in brief statements, they suggest how their lists were useful or not useful.

Following are two examples of checklists that students can use to write essays and short stories.

Checklist for Developing More Genuine Characters

- How does she dress?
- What does he eat?
- Is she healthy or sickly?
- What does he do in his spare time? What would he like to do?
- Where does she work? Does she enjoy her work? Why?
- If he had three wishes what would they be? Why?
- What are her habits?
- Who are his parents? Siblings? Relatives?
- Does she smoke? What? Why?
- Does he drink? When? How much?
- Is she athletic? How?
- Does he have romance in his life? Who? How long?
- Has she difficulties, strange behaviors, or problems?
- What are his dreams, hopes, ambitions, fears?
- Is she well educated? In what? Where? How?
- How much money does he have? Why? Is he tightfisted? Generous?
- Where does she live? In what sort of home?
- Who are his best friends? His enemies?
- What does she think about books, travel, music, gardening, culture, romance, hockey?
- What is his race? Religion? Nationality?
- What is her worldview? Why?
- Are his social and political views common?
- What are her wildest opinions? Why?
- How much traveling has he done? Where? Why?
- How does she react to war? Children? Peers? Thunderstorms? Hurricanes? Rain? Sarcasm? Laughter?

Checklist for Editing a First Draft

- Does your topic interest you?

- If not, reword your title until you are interested.

- Are paragraphs short (3 or 4 sentences)?

- Are sentences short (fewer than 11 words)?

- How about a few very short sentences (1 to 3 words)?

- Does each sentence in the paragraph relate to the first?

- Are all words spelled correctly?

- Did you show things as if on a movie screen?

- Did you cross out all extra words?

- Write your main idea in one brief, clear sentence.

- Do all ideas relate to the one main idea?

- Does the first sentence hook the reader?

- Does the final sentence sum up what the first began?

- Will readers go away satisfied?

- Are all topic sentences in logical order? (You might read aloud the first sentence in each paragraph to check.)

- Read your essay or story out loud or into a tape. Have you left any gaps?

ACTIVITY 5.2 Interview a Famous Figure

Outcome
A role-played interview of a character

Discussion and Procedure
In groups of three, students choose two men or women from the lesson to research. Students read more about the characters, using library books, magazines, and the Internet. They discuss their research with other members of the group. They consider how each character might respond to similar problems or challenges today. They create a meeting of the characters and role-play an interview in which one character interviews the other. Students reverse roles. They may prepare taped TV or radio interviews to present their interviews to the class.

Following is a list of questions students might come up in a scenario in which Canadian Prime Minister Paul Martin might ask Martin Luther King Jr. about racism.

1. What motivated you to stick your neck out for others?

2. What was your family life like?

3. Who were your best friends?

4. Where did you find support, encouragement, or comfort when others opposed you?

5. If you were granted one wish today, what would it be?

6. What could Canadian politicians learn from your life?

7. What kind of schools would you like to see for your grandchildren and their children?

8. What contributes most to racism today?

9. Is racial intolerance less evident today, or is it as serious as it was when you were alive?

10. How can we create a greater love among youth of every culture?

11. What presents the major barriers to caring and cooperation among the nations?

12. If you could pass on one key message to this generation, what would that message be?

ACTIVITY 5.3   Record Insights Gained

Outcome

An insight sheet on which are recorded insights and discoveries gained in a class, reading, group activity, or project

Discussion and Procedure

You might ask the following questions to help students understand world hunger:

- What are your personal experiences with hunger?

- What kinds of world hunger besides physical hunger exist?

- What similarities are there between hunger in inner cities and hunger in the suburbs?

- What are your ideas for solutions?

- Who should solve the problems? How?

- What are the obstacles?

Have students create their own insight sheets using art, symbols, or colors. At the end of an instructional unit, after a test, or following a difficult experiment, students record valuable ideas from the work and insights that they want to take with them. In groups of three or four, they discuss their insights and consider possible arguments for other alternative views. They briefly record alternative ideas. They refer to their sheets over time to keep track of their own thinking and progressively develop new insights.

Following is a sample of one student's responses on an insight sheet:

Insights I Discovered for Successful Ways to Bring about Change
(My insights were generated from a process of working with teachers, students, and parents of many different cultures and in many different settings.)

- Initiate change in small increments—geographically, technologically, and conceptually.

- Help others by doing projects with them, by working alongside.

- Respect human dignity. Draw on experience and knowledge of each one in the group.

- Achieve innovation at minimum cost by using local resources.

- Complete all tasks with excellence. Assess and evaluate.

- Share what you have learned with others. Ideas not shared have no value.

- Create satisfaction—both personal and group.

- Base innovation on wisdom, not mere knowledge. Many believe the process of lasting change is a spiritual one, not merely an intellectual one.

You may wish to have students brainstorm questions that will generate significant information. You may wish to list places that students might look for information. Or you may brainstorm a list of topics related to the main theme, and groups or individuals may choose their research topic from the list. The students then research the ideas and, at various times along the way, gather to discuss and debate their findings.

ACTIVITY 5.4   Defending Facts

Facts	Arguments

Outcome
A T-chart to consider both sides of an issue

Discussion and Procedure
Students research the facts about their issue. They list the main facts on the left in the T-chart under an appropriate title. In groups of three or four, they discuss the facts and consider possible arguments for an alternative view. They briefly list the arguments on the right side of the T-chart. After discussing the facts and arguments, they prepare to defend one side or the other for each fact listed.

Students may be quizzed on some facts, debate the main issues, or present a musical to depict what has been done to resolve the problem. The idea is to provide opportunities for students to practice a variety of skills.

ACTIVITY 5.5   Problem-Solving Paths

Outcome
A problem-solving graphic

Discussion and Procedure
Students write down a problem to be solved and list reasons for the problem. They name the person or group that will be most affected by this problem. They outline several solutions that may work to solve the problem. They explore the possible results the suggested solutions will have and identify the best solution for this problem.

ACTIVITY 5.6   A Project Using at Least Five Intelligences

Outcome
A project design using at least five of Gardener's eight intelligences

Discussion and Procedure

Students design a project that uses at least five of the eight intelligences to present their information. Students can meet in groups of five to brainstorm ideas for a project whose results can be expressed in a variety of ways. Students might build interactive display centers to demonstrate their work. The following ideas may provide a springboard for a project on world hunger.

Eight Centers to Display Projects

1. **Bodily-Kinesthetic: Building Center.** Construct a typical community in Calcutta. Design this site after brainstorming ideas about poor communities in India and other nonindustrialized nations.

2. **Mathematical-Logical: Math Center.** Using numbers in a meaningful configuration, resolve problems about unequal distribution, budgeting, and money ratios. Create a graph showing where most problems are concentrated.

3. **Verbal-Linguistic: Reading Center.** Write a story about money, world markets, banking, and world hunger. Display your stories on the bulletin board. Write and publish a letter to the editor of the local newspaper on world hunger and big business problems. Suggest a solution.

4. **Musical-Rhythmic: Music Center.** Play music that reflects world hunger problems and solutions. Write a song to express the group's emotions about the problems and solutions.

5. **Visual-Spatial: Art Center.** Design architectural plans for the re-creation of poor communities. In a wall collage, show good banking principles. Portray current poverty and possible solutions in nonindustrialized countries. Display photographs of an inner-city ghetto to tell a story.

6. **Interpersonal: Working-Together Center.** Discuss and solve banking problems cooperatively. Create role-plays that depict banking practices and debate controversial money issues, answering questions jointly.

7. **Intrapersonal: Personal Center.** Create your own responses to the world hunger problem and provide solutions. Share your work with the class to get feedback.

8. **Naturalistic: Nature Center.** Create a museum that illustrates nature's part in problems and possibilities related to world hunger. List and illustrate five creative examples or solutions that a naturalist might suggest to overcome world hunger.

Students enjoy working cooperatively to create learning centers for their display. Groups then teach one another about their specialty. The outside community enjoys visiting the learning centers. Through this work, students learn more about themselves and about their own community.

By working in groups, these students develop their own unique gifts and strengthen each group's collective abilities to know artistically, mathematically, musically, linguistically, kinesthetically, interpersonally, and independently.

CONSTRUCTIVIST LEARNING APPROACHES

Constructivists Lev Vygotsky, John Dewey, and Jean Piaget have described learning as a creation of meaning—or when a person connects new knowledge to existing knowledge. They believed that a person "constructs" personal knowledge within community, usually through interchanges with others.

Constructivism differs from the traditional, reductionist approach, which has shaped education in North American schools for generations. The reductionist paradigm is deficit driven and presupposes that learners must break concepts into small segments or steps. Students must learn lower-order skills before they learn higher-order skills in a kind of hierarchical progression. By accumulating isolated facts, learners are expected to build skills and generate new knowledge.

Constructivism, in contrast, suggests that people are learning constantly. Constructivism takes into account the learner's unique abilities, knowledge, faith, and past experiences.

ACTIVITY 5.7 | Make a Jelly Sandwich

Outcome
A jelly sandwich for each student

Discussion and Procedure
This activity enables students to construct and follow directions. It provides an enjoyable opportunity to explain a concrete situation from their own experiences. If done in a spirit of fun, the activity will not embarrass students.

Have students write out directions for making a jelly sandwich as if intended for a person who had never made one. After all students' recipes are completed, set up several work stations, with jars of jelly, plates, knives, and two slices of bread for each student. Divide the students into pairs and have the members of each pair exchange recipes. Remind students to wash their hands before handling food, and then instruct them to make a sandwich, following their partners' instructions exactly. Students cannot ask for any help from their partners.

When students have finished making sandwiches, they exchange sandwiches and eat their results. If directions were clear, they will be handed a well-prepared jelly sandwich. For those students who rushed through the exercise or who left large gaps in directions, the poorly made sandwiches will illustrate the problems and provide concrete evidence of the problems we encounter in everyday written directions.

ACTIVITY 5.8 | Introduce a New Poem to Your Group

Outcome
A meaningful poem or speech presented to the group using several of the intelligences

Discussion and Procedure

In groups of three or four, students each choose a poem or speech and present it to their groups using several of the intelligences. The presentations might include the following:

1. **Logical-mathematical:** List five main ideas in sequence. You may wish to illustrate several of the main events on a poster or through personal illustrations.

2. **Verbal-linguistic:** Read the poem or speech a few times just to enjoy it and get a feeling for the language. Prepare to read the selection aloud to the group to dramatize its main message. You may wish to add background music to accompany your recitation.

3. **Musical-rhythmic:** Choose a musical selection that expresses the mood of the poem or speech. You may wish to create your own music.

4. **Visual-spatial:** Create a tableau to illustrate the poem or speech. You may wish to emphasize one main theme. Background music may help to create the best mood for your tableau.

5. **Bodily-kinesthetic:** Create a dance in order to tell the poem's story or to illustrate the main message of the speech.

6. **Interpersonal:** Create a crossword puzzle with a partner. Use ideas from the selection and from your research on its theme.

7. **Intrapersonal:** Read the poem or speech two or three times. Then write a few paragraphs about an event or thought that this selection generates from your own life.

8. **Naturalistic:** Show how nature impacts one event in your day and suggest how the natural world enhances creativity within each of us.

Encourage students to enjoy poetry rather than dissecting it. Students choose one or two group presentations to share with the entire class. Activities might be displayed on the bulletin board or presented to the group. After participating in a variety of activities, students may compare their ideas and discuss the variations. Students may wish to write their own poetry on the same or a similar topic.

ACTIVITY 5.9   Feedback Sheets

Outcome

A feedback form used at regular intervals to provide feedback about the positive features of a course and offer suggestions for possible changes

Discussion and Procedure

When students first attempt to bring their uniqueness to a new unit taught, some may experience difficulty. In this case, reflection sheets, like those on the next page, are valuable.

Community-Building Approaches

Learning centers encourage community cooperation in several ways. In smaller groups, students are freer to express their ideas and get help with difficult problems. The classroom community is strengthened as each small group teaches the

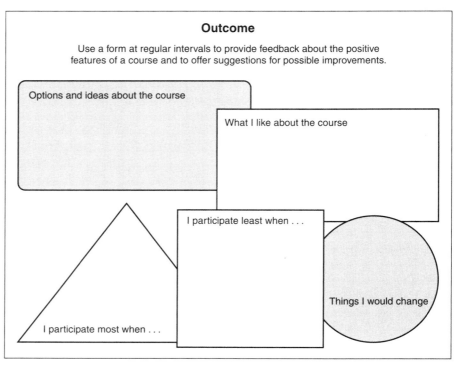

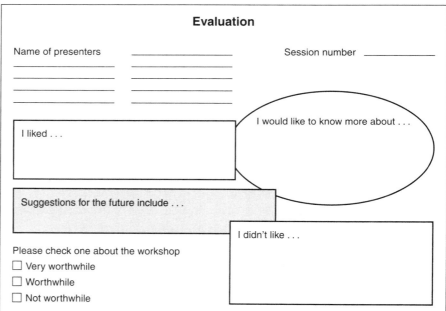

rest of the class. The larger community is united when students present their work to the community and engage with parents, grandparents, and other visitors.

In community-based activities, learners vary in age, gender, ability, ethnicity, and interests. Community-based activities may include immediate family, extended family, or community members. They may also include only the learners; Kasten and Clarke (1993) define a classroom community as "any deliberate

grouping of children that includes more than one traditional grade level" (p. 45). I amend their definition to "any deliberate multigrade grouping of learners who seek to solve problems or create products together in a roundtable setting." Community activities capitalize on the diverse knowledge and abilities of many team players. While community learning is not yet a norm for North American schools, the image of a roundtable approach to learning is gaining more attention from both adults and youth.

The key to community learning is shared power. Villa and Thousand (1992) suggest that educators model collaboration by sharing their decision-making and teaching power with students. In roundtable learning, teachers welcome students as partners on the planning, teaching, and learning team. They mediate conflicts that deter successful learning. They support peers and expect to be supported. They influence their teachers as reciprocal learners and teachers and thus affect policy guiding their learning endeavors.

Following are suggested activities for community learning in a unit on world hunger:

1. **Building Center.** Students compare and contrast communities. They consider values and traditions that will determine how their structures will be built.

2. **Math Center.** Students solve problems and consider as a group how various communities work to feed their families.

3. **Reading Center.** Students write and share stories about community and relate their ideas about world hunger issues.

4. **Music Center.** Students build a music library based on collective emotions and discuss community ideas about world hunger problems.

5. **Art Center.** Students design architectural plans for remodeling poor communities. They consider realistic ways in which needy communities might restructure to take advantage of more resources.

6. **Working-Together Center.** Students discuss and solve banking problems cooperatively, answering questions about community development and financial resource management.

7. **Personal Center.** Students create personal responses that they share. Sharing allows students to correct mistakes and add new insights.

8. **Natural Center.** Students compare and contrast communities situated in diverse environments. They show the impact on life and learning for others their own age.

In each activity, students learn in community and solve real-life community problems.

A ROUNDTABLE APPROACH TO TEACHING A UNIT ON SHORT STORIES

The purpose of this two-week unit is to engage students in a variety of activities that focus on reading and writing short stories and on the building of community. Students respond to short stories through reading, storytelling, role-play, written projects, music, and art. This unit emphasizes the fact that we write stories in various ways and that within community we can share stories and receive constructive criticism. The following list highlights the purposes of the unit:

- to respond to a variety of stories from literature and personal experience
- to participate in storytelling in small groups
- to write stories from past experiences or personal interests
- to express stories through role-play, music, and art
- to list collaboratively the parts of a short story
- to develop a checklist for creating vivid characters
- to edit one another's short stories

Question First, Teach Later

When you raise critical questions, discussions about content grow lively and interesting. Students explore various ideas through well-developed questions. The questions activate their unique learning abilities to respond to their own inquiries. The secret for maintaining high student participation and enthusiasm is to encourage questions that allow learners to express a deep understanding of each new topic. Gardner (1991) suggests that teachers also consider how students might be grouped according to diverse abilities to solve problems or create a new product in each lesson. I have learned over my many years of teaching that students already have developed their unique ideas about many topics. Questioning helps you facilitate their knowledge and challenge their thinking further.

Opportunities for Assessment

Activities in this unit provide many opportunities for teachers, peers, and students themselves to evaluate learning. Each activity has a guide to assessment. Each guide suggests a variety of areas to assess, and specific criteria and indicators are included. The unit also has a guide to assessment as well as a form for teacher, student, and parent comments.

ACTIVITY 5.10   ## Use of Literature and Personal Experiences

Procedure

Ask questions to hook students' interests to "The Schoolmistress" by Anton Chekhov. Here are some questions you might use:

1. Think about an interesting teacher. What did she or he do? What did she or he look like?

2. What was your first school like? How many different schools have you attended?

3. Will you take your children to see your schools? Why or why not?

4. What did your school look like? What did it feel like to belong?

5. What did you like best about your school?

6. What did you like least?

7. What route did you take to the school? How did you travel? What did you see along the way?

8. Describe how you felt as you traveled to school on a typical morning.

9. Does anybody know what a Russian school was like about twenty years ago?

Then read "The Schoolmistress" together with students out loud and in parts. Discuss or define any words students don't know as you go, or have students write down such words to look up later.

Assignment

Ask each student to bring one interesting fact about Chekhov to class tomorrow that might increase the class's enjoyment of this story. Piece his life and work into a mural for the bulletin board, and show the story's main themes as they relate to students today.

Assessment

Self-assessment reflection can relate to reading and understanding the text, using the following questions as a guide:

1. I found it hard to listen when . . .

2. When someone is talking, I usually . . .

3. It's hard to remember what is said when . . .

4. The parts I enjoyed listening to most were . . .

5. When I must remember something I've heard, I . . .

6. I listen best when . . .

ACTIVITY 5.11 Storytelling in Small Groups Using a Talking Stick

Procedure

In groups of three or four, have students tell a story about some school experience they have had. They can make up parts of the story from their imagination, but they should weave the story from a true incident. Use the talking stick (or other object) to pass from one student who is talking to the next.

Assessment

The following questions can help guide self-assessment:

1. What story did you tell?

2. Were you a better talker, listener, or a bit of both? Why do you think so?

3. Who shared a story first? Last? How did your group decide who would take the next turn?

4. What do you believe it takes to make a group work well together?

5. Tell us about some other experiences you had with group work?

6. What was you best experience in the group?

7. What was your worst experience in the group?

8. How do you think this group work should be evaluated? As a group? As individuals?

9. How do you indicate to the group that you are listening?

10. Do you lead in a group or prefer others to lead?

11. Is there anything else you would like to add about your contribution to the group?

ACTIVITY 5.12 Writing a Personal Story

Procedure

Students begin to write the stories they told in the circles. Tell them to keep writing for ten minutes without stopping. They should not lift the pen or pencil from the page because you will assess them, in part, on whether they continued writing without a break. Even if they merely repeat the sentence "I can't think of anything to say," they should not stop writing until you call time.

Assessment

Tell students these original writings will be passed in with a copy of their final draft. They will be marked up and messy, but they will probably contain the ideas to be used in the final version.

ACTIVITY 5.13 Organizing Your Written Ideas

Procedure

This activity helps develop logical intelligence. The process is divided into three steps: prewriting, writing, and editing.

1. **Prewriting:** Students choose and write down working titles for their short stories. (*Working title* means they may change it later.) Using the rough notes from Activity 5.14, they list five major ideas under the title. They add minor ideas under each of the five main ideas. All ideas may be actual sentences pulled from the rough notes. They then assemble these in an order that tells a good story.

2. **Writing:** Using these notes as a guide, students write meaningful sentences that move the reader from one event to the next. Suggest they use such transitions as *then, whenever, however, nonetheless,* and *therefore* to connect the five sections.

3. **Editing:** Remind students that they don't have to get it right the first time! They should use the checklist in Activity 5.17 to polish their words and ideas. You might compare this process to polishing a magic lamp—the genie of their best ideas leaps out to the reader.

Assessment

Tell students to save and number their prewriting, writing, and editing copies to pass in with the final story. They should write a brief explanation of how they used each stage to create the final story.

ACTIVITY 5.14   Share the Story with Group

The next step is for the students to tell their stories to an audience without using words. Challenge them to create a work of art, a sound track, or mime to relate the story to the class in a meaningful way. The audience must get some sense of what each story is about.

Assessment

Invite parents and knowledgeable community members to write critiques of the presentations. Have them sign their critiques. You might have them answer the following questions:

1. How did this work express the story?

2. Was the mood obvious?

3. What additional methods would have worked?

4. Were the characters and plot well delineated? Were they interesting?

5. Was the plot movement clear?

6. Was the work creative? Original? High quality?

7. On a scale of 1 to 10, with 10 being best, what mark would you assign this work?

ACTIVITY 5.15   Collaborating to Identify Parts of a Story

Procedure

Have students form groups of three or four to consider Chekhov's story and the stories written by their classmates. Ask them to list the main parts of any good story. Have them think of a story that knits the distinct pieces of action to form action on a larger scale. Ask them if there is a theme through the story. A short story usually relates one single incident, with color and imagination. Ask them which of the five senses Chekhov's story uses. In other words, when they read the story, did they see, touch, taste, smell, or hear? Should all stories appeal to all five of our senses?

Assessment

Have the students answer the following questions to help in self-assessment:

1. Did you contribute any parts to a story?

2. How many short stories do you read in a week? In a month? Would you rather read or watch TV?

3. Do you usually understand what you read?

4. Do you have a public library card? Do you use that library or the school library regularly?

5. What kind of stories do you usually read?

6. Do you consider yourself a good reader?

7. Do you read as well as you'd like to?

8. What was the last story you read outside this class? When?

9. Where do you find most of your stories?

10. What would you like to do to improve your reading?

ACTIVITY 5.16   Discuss Characters

Procedure

Pass out the following checklist to each student. Allow students time in small groups to discuss the list and to add six additional significant questions. You may wish to list their questions on the board. After you discuss the list, assign students the task of asking and answering the questions about characters they created.

Students may ask some of the following questions:

1. Do we really know much detail about the main character's lifestyle?

2. What details helped to move the story along? How?

3. Which details are not critically related to the story's plot?

   In addition, students might ask and answer these questions:

   • What does the character wear?

   • What friends does the character have?

   • What foods does the character prefer?

   • How does the character style her or his hair?

   • What is the exact state of the character's health?

   • Is there anything distinctive about the character's language or use of language?

   • Was the character chosen to lead? Why?

   • Does the character have any hobbies? What are they?

   • What work does the character do? Does he or she like it?

   • When did the character start smoking?

- What does the character try to get away with? Why does the character think he or she can?

- Is the character athletic? In what way?

- Who likes the character? Does the character have any romantic relationship?

- When did the character leave home? Why?

- Why does the character act superior?

- Whom does the character date?

- How much education does the character have?

- In what ways is the character biased against other people?

- What are the character's dreams? Hopes? Ambitions? Fears?

- What religion does the character practice?

- How does the character treat enemies?

- What is the character's philosophy about life?

- How much traveling has the character done? To what places?

- What are the character's reactions to tears? To treachery? To heat? To sarcasm?

- What is the character's race or nationality?

- How much money does the character have?

- What does the character think about books? Music? Flowers?

Students will add five questions to the list as part of a personal guideline to create vivid stories.

ACTIVITY 5.17   Edit Stories

Procedure

Students use the following questions to find problems in their stories. Then they refine their stories.

- Does the topic interest you?

- How would you reword the title so that you like it?

- Does the opening sentence hook your reader?

- Are your paragraphs short and focused? (Ordinarily, they should be three or four sentences. Although you may have longer paragraphs, they should not all be long.)

- Are your sentences short (under 11 words)?

- Do you have a few short, sharp sentences (1 to 3 words)?

- Does each sentence in a paragraph relate to its opening sentence?

- Did you show things as if on stage?

- Did you omit all extra words?
- Did you use a dictionary to check your spelling?
- Can you write your main idea in one brief sentence?
- Have you thrown out any ideas not related to the main idea?
- Does you last sentence sum up what the first began?
- Will your reader go away satisfied?
- Are topic sentences in logical order? (Read aloud the first sentence in each paragraph to check.)
- Are your characters real?
- Did you let your characters talk to one another?
- When you read your story aloud or onto a tape, are there any gaps?
- What would a good friend say about your story?
- Have you word processed your story and saved it?

Assessment

Have students use questions such as the following to assess their work:

1. What changes did you make to the story?
2. Have you discussed your changes in your group and described how your story changed?
3. Are there other changes you should make?
4. What changes do you plan to make to improve your story?

ACTIVITY 5.18   Create Readings for Community Members

Procedure and Assessment

One student writes a school newspaper article about another student's reading. Ask students whether they agree with the article. Why or why not?

ACTIVITY 5.19   Publish Short Stories

Procedure and Assessment

Using the checklists and considering the self-assessment forms, have students respond to four areas of growth and achievement:

1. **Work and study habits.** You might record attentiveness, cooperation, dependability, self-discipline, initiative, enthusiasm, attendance, punctuality, organization, and use of oral language (small-group learning, speaking, and listening).
2. **Speaking.** You might record attitude, content, organization, expression, role-playing, and helpfulness to other writers.
3. **Listening.** You might record attitude, evidences, responsiveness, and applications of suggestions.

4. **Writing and editing.** You might record attitude, composing and creating, revising, and incorporating peer suggestions.

5. **Final product.** The summative evaluation might include a culmination of tests, examinations, and projects completed and filed throughout this unit.

I strongly recommend that you set goals with students and select certain criteria for assessment before each activity begins. Students often become discouraged if they are expected to improve in too many areas at once. Note progress and record some assessment for each activity.

Additional Opportunities for Integrating the Unit in the Community

The following list has some ideas for integration throughout the community. Collaboration with people of Russian origin or experience with authors would provide opportunities for learning about short stories.

1. Invite a writer to come to conduct a Saturday morning short story workshop. Offer extra credit for those who attend and have them report to the class.

2. Have students tape-record an interview with a person about some aspect of his or her life. Students should collaborate on interview questions. Discuss with them how real-life events provide interesting plots for short stories.

3. Set up a room for several students to read their short stories. Provide background music and serve refreshments to those who attend.

4. Ask students to create art that illustrates the stories and display their artwork. Discuss projects and learn how each work relates to the theme.

5. Students can stage stories by creating three-act plays. Invite community members to the final production.

6. Have students use a word processor to compile several short stories into a book to sell to the community.

7. Students can create tests for those who have read their short stories. Have them test a small group following a reading. They should revise the test if needed.

HOW ARE YOU SMART? TEST YOURSELF

Early on in my career I had the good fortune of working with a community leader who refused to label people. "People who are smart in business are not always good teachers," he would say. And most people agree that we are smart in many ways and that these differ depending on our intellectual blueprints and on life experiences. What we enjoy or excel in today may not be the same tomorrow. Through the following surveys, we can identify special strengths, and we grow stronger in ways that add new tools for facing old challenges. Sift through the surveys in this section and complete only the ones that offer you answers that will work today.

This brain-based survey allows you to identify strengths as well as weaker abilities. According to Caroline Sutherland, author of *The Body Knows* (2001), scientific research has now documented links between many of the obstacles we face in life, such as depression and stress, to organs related to the immune system, such as the thymus, spleen, lymph, and adrenal glands. We know more about how we can help these links work to help us prosper in life, and we know that every cell we have holds a component of our immunity blueprint encoded within it. A strong mental system creates a stronger immune system. When we identify our strengths and weaknesses, we begin to align our heads, hearts, and bodies for the full health that many only dream of. We add balance to brain parts that sustain success.

In this section of the book, you will discover that parts of your brain may be working at cross-purposes to a healthy lifestyle. Here you can find out what you are born to do in life, and you then can adjust the circumstances of your life based on new or suppressed talents you will uncover. You will not only discover pathways past stress and depression, but will find hidden strengths that will add missing puzzle pieces to help you prosper you on a daily basis.

Survey for Discovering Your Strongest Intelligences

If you start this survey with an open mind—by that I mean that you come to it wanting to look inside the real you—then you will leave with life-altering answers. I've never encountered a person who, when they pursued a deep question, did not find some solutions that work well. Beatrice is one who comes to mind. When I worked with her on Baffin Island, she asked, "How can I escape the blues I feel every day at work?" Beatrice resented others who did well and made money from their businesses; she found herself locked out of their fun and friendships.

After several questions, and when she saw her strengths after taking this survey during one of my sessions, she left the Arctic for a lighter climate. It turned out that Beatrice had let go of her love for music and dance. Darkness that covers Arctic skies for four months at a time had blinded the parts of her brain that brought her success and satisfaction. I met Beatrice a few years later at a conference at McGill, and she had recovered quite well. She still struggles during Maine's darker days, but she runs a dance studio and no longer lives without using her talents. Like many setbacks we face, this was a mental barrier and was deeply imprinted in the fabric of the mind.

On the following list, check at least fifteen statements that best capture your unique interests and abilities. This survey works best when you let intuitions about your life speak to each survey item without stopping to analyze the value of any one issue addressed. A steady pace of answering will help you to identify strengths that others would validate also; this is where we begin to build better techniques for daily living. When you are finished taking the quiz, review the key to determine your strongest intelligences.

_____ 1. It's often hard for me to sit still. I'd rather be up and active.

_____ 2. I often organize a time schedule to plan my week.

_____ 3. I enjoy taking great photographs.

_____ 4. Designing a Web page would be a good challenge to me.

_____ 5. I enjoy throwing-and-catching games.

_____ 6. I would love to design an advertisement.

_____ 7. Preparing to debate an issue is a challenge I enjoy.

_____ 8. Sometimes I find myself tapping rhythms on a table.

_____ 9. Telling stories to a group is a lot of fun.

_____ 10. For me, sketching a building seems easier than baking a cake.

_____ 11. When working in a group, I like to summarize people's ideas.

_____ 12. Multiple-choice tests are usually easy for me.

_____ 13. Someday I'd like to join a march to show my concern for others.

_____ 14. I have always wanted to learn to play guitar.

_____ 15. I like to write about a special day or an adventure.

_____ 16. As I read, I make more sense of the text by outlining chapters.

_____ 17. Choosing the best metaphor in a poem is a joy for me.

_____ 18. I love to participate on a team.

_____ 19. When dining in a restaurant, I enjoy the background music.

_____ 20. Sometimes I like to go for a walk all alone.

_____ 21. When I read a novel, I often compare personal choices I make.

_____ 22. Reading a map, I easily find my destination.

_____ 23. After a concert, I hear the melodies in my mind for days.

_____ 24. When I catch fish, I love to clean them and cook them on a campfire.

_____ 25. I enjoy singing in the choir, even when my week is very busy.

_____ 26. When I write, I tend to base my stories on personal experience.

_____ 27. I easily identify patterns and see larger meanings in small data.

_____ 28. I learn from and enjoy nature's changes during each season.

_____ 29. I do my best thinking when brainstorming with others.

_____ 30. Helping others to complete a project is very satisfying.

_____ 31. Finding solutions for numerical problems is fun.

_____ 32. I would enjoy collaborating on writing a joint press release.

_____ 33. Every chance I get, I play golf, tennis, or softball.

_____ 34. I would love the challenge of acting in a play.

_____ 35. I like to learn more about me in interest inventories.

_____ 36. I enjoy learning new dances and moving to music.

_____ 37. As I walk in the woods, I often pause to observe the wildlife.

_____ 38. I am drawn to any place with water—lakes, rivers, or oceans.

_____ 39. I would enjoy writing an essay for a contest.

_____ 40. Sometimes I get up early to go outside and watch the sunrise.

Answers are sorted by each intelligence, as follows:

Verbal-linguistic: 7, 9, 11, 15, 17, 39

Mathematical-logical: 2, 12, 16, 27, 31

Visual-spatial: 3, 4, 6, 10, 22

Musical-rhythmic: 8, 14, 19, 23, 25

Bodily-kinesthetic: 1, 5, 33, 34, 36

Interpersonal: 13, 18, 29, 30, 32

Intrapersonal: 5, 20, 21, 26, 35

Naturalistic: 24, 28, 37, 38, 40

Your score is probably evenly distributed across several areas, but you will note one or two areas that have more scores; perhaps one of the intelligences did not have any scores. Select the three intelligences on which you scored the fewest points. It is helpful to focus your energies on at least one of these weaker areas. You are free to work on all of the intelligences, but you will benefit most noticeably if you focus on the areas in which you are currently deficient.

You may believe that your weakest areas are attributes that are not important in your life. You see that you have come this far without focusing on them, and you think that you might well live your whole life without tapping into these parts of your brain. However, when you begin to explore your overlooked talents, you begin to see how you can be transformed into the more successful person you'd rather be.

Hold onto your students' profiles that they complete, as you will use their survey scores to help them move through roundtable activities that are illustrated in this book and that you create within faculty planning circles. Throughout the book, you have observed that intelligent people approach life and growth by unleashing new parts of their brains. You'll see your students in a new light within the roundtable, and you will find creative opportunities to identify, test, and develop new intelligences that will make you view life in innovative ways.

WHAT EFFECT DOES MUSIC HAVE ON LEARNING?

Music can make students smarter. There are ways to use music as a background cadence that can aid deeper understanding. Music can shift our brain waves so that we accomplish more from even ordinary events, whether it is reading, walking, sharing lunch with a friend, or taking on a challenging new project at home or work.

Students can physically speed up thought or slow it down to plunge deeper into insight. In addition, each of the eight intelligences can stimulate brain waves. Physically active people sense, for example, that going for a twenty-minute run can make them feel powerfully refreshed. In fact, they have simply altered their brain waves. Nature-oriented people might achieve this effect by going for a canoe ride, and verbal people can refresh themselves by having a spirited conversation at a book group. Psychologist Don Campbell revealed how music can alter our mental states. His book *The Mozart Effect* (2001) suggests that the following music types may affect the listener in these ways:

- Gregorian chants create quiet in our minds and can reduce stress.

- Slower Baroque music, such as Bach, Handel, Vivaldi, or Corelli, can create mentally stimulating environments for creativity and new innovations.

- Classical music, such as Haydn and Mozart, often improves concentration and memory when played in the background.

- Romantic music, such as Schubert, Schumann, Tchaikovsky, Chopin, and Liszt, enhances our senses and increases a sense of sympathy and love.

- Impressionist music, such as Debussy, Fauré, and Ravel, can unlock dreamlike images that put us in touch with our unconscious thoughts and belief systems.

- Jazz, blues, soul, or calypso music can uplift and inspire us, releasing deep joy or even deep sadness, conveying wit and affirming our common humanity.

- Salsa, rhumba, merengue, and any form of South American music sets our hearts racing, gets us moving, both relaxing us and awakening us at the same time.

- Big band, top 40, and country music engage our emotions and comfort us.

- Rock music, from Elvis Presley to the Rolling Stones, stirs passion and activity and so can release daily tensions. Rock can also mask pain and cover up unpleasant noises. It also has the power to create dissonance, stress, or physical pain if we are not in the mood for energizing.

- Ambient or New Age music, such as Stephen Halpern and Brian Eno, has no dominant rhythm, and so it elongates the sense of space and time, inducing a state of relaxed alertness.

- Heavy metal and hip-hop music excite our nervous system and sometimes lead us into acting out dynamic behavior and self-expression.

- Religious and sacred music, such as hymns and gospel, moves us to feel grounded in the moment and leads to deep peace and spiritual awareness. Sacred music often helps us to transcend pain.

Students will often be more open to listening to various musical types when they understand how music impacts their learning. Rather than give them lists and tell them what to expect, why not play on low volume a variety of musical selections as background to their work and ask their opinions of what the music did to help or hinder their progress. Get many ideas and listen carefully to students, since many differences will be articulated. This can provide an opportunity to help students to find the music that works best for them in various situations.

Not surprisingly, since their brains have formed patterns already in relation to how music impacts their learning and since their brains are all wired differently, you can expect to hear a wide variety of responses. Insights garnered as a result of the exchanges and the listening exercises will create an excellent basis for discussion. This is an ideal time to build a classroom consensus about how to use music to help learning, based on what students have learned about their brains and about music's ability to change brain waves. Many teachers use this opportunity to build community, with the added dimension of music in the background, and to collaborate with students to create innovative settings that benefit many students in their circles.

CHAPTER 6

Roundtables in Times of Change

Things do not change; we change.

Henry David Thoreau, *Walden*

This chapter suggests creative activities that challenge faculty and students to succeed together in an atmosphere of change within today's schools and within our society. One constant is that change is inevitable. When changes are embraced for the sake of higher motivation and achievement, the entire community benefits. It is rarely easy to do this. Adjusting to the change takes time, and faculty can find themselves frustrated by increasing daily time demands. Whether it is having more students in a class, new technology programs to learn, more paperwork, or extra committee work, faculty often experience change more as another add on to their already hectic lives than as a benefit.

Sometimes change feels lonely, and the way to improvement can appear uncertain. In spite of the uncertainties of change, when faculty "start at the end" to motivate students, they can stimulate creative and productive energy in the class. To "start at the end," you describe for yourself and others the end results you envision for a lesson, a class, or roundtable support circle. Then you live daily as if that end were close at hand. For many faculty, to start at the end, and to envision specific results, is to free students and others to take the risks required before improvements take place.

Those who learn to work within and help to shape the direction of change will survive the waves and sail into calmer waters. Roundtables are designed to support one another in times of change. The learning circles described here are intended to help both faculty and students to shape and refine changes, which can result in quality learning.

Along the way we can learn from the pros—by observing them, seeking them out as mentors, and inviting them into classes as partners. Just as we seek the help of masters in the field, we should also remain mindful that some professionals become complacent and stagnate. In contrast, we can embrace the brain-based learning opportunities in any roundtable to encourage all participants in an evolution forward.

CHANGING CULTURES INTO
CARING COMMUNITIES

In order to cultivate faith in ourselves as learners, we must find a safe environment for our students to learn to lead with their strengths. This is not easy in the midst of the many changes taking place in our schools. Renewal opportunities in this book relate to using more resources within our students rather than a call for extra resources from outside the schools. Creative roundtable learning usually starts with teachers who are willing to take personal risks, become vulnerable, and learn with their students. To build circles where strengths create the fastest way to genius, we often step out of former comfort zones or places of isolation. We look to courageous facilitators. All the great ideas and visions in your circle do not require another chief organizer. Brain-based leadership often requires courageous disorganizers.

Safe environments and caring communities do not presuppose classrooms without change. Safety is generated by creating clear standards and guidance toward personal and communal goals. Only after teachers and parents accept their own shortcomings and abilities can they muster courage to help students respond to changes. These changes might involve gender roles and may require you to enter roles not typically assigned to your circle. Why wait for official blessing to try new things? To be prudent in leading change is to avoid naysayers who view their job as to say no to innovations. In contrast, if they haven't explicitly been told no, brain-based leaders try.

If you look past assumptions, you tend to find people who make a difference in any learning circle. For years, many of us have heard the expression, "If it isn't broke, don't fix it." In the face of many improvements required in schools today, this saying seems to be more a slogan of complacency, arrogance, or fear. Furthermore, it develops a mind-set that assumes that today's realities will contain tomorrow's best, in tidy, linear, and predictable ways. This is sheer fantasy!

In safe and caring communities, students expect to accomplish more. They sense that people are the highest currency, that leaders immerse themselves in human assets. For this reason, the best, brightest, most creative ideas are attracted, retained, and, most importantly, unleashed. Change requires students and faculty to accomplish things never before accomplished, by using parts of the brain never before used.

In the tasks that follow, your students will integrate ideas from multiple intelligences, problem solving, human diversity, differentiation, social justice, intelligence-fair assessments, reflective thinking, and equity. The goal is to practice approaches that have roots in current theories about how to garner more from the human brain.

ACTIVITY 6.1   Male-Female Circle—Identifying Stereotypes in Music

Outcome

A collage to express discoveries of male and female stereotypes in selections of music

Discussion and Procedure

Students choose several musical selections from Campbell's lists in *The Mozart Effect* (2001), as discussed in Chapter 5. Campbell suggests that different kinds of music create different mental effects. These are only suggestions, that certain kinds of music might encourage certain tendencies. Campbell suggests, that the following music types may have these effects:

- *Gregorian chants* can help quiet study and reduce stress.

- *Slower Baroque music* (such as Bach, Handel, Vivaldi, Corelli) can create a mentally stimulating environment for creativity or study.

- *Classical music* (Haydn and Mozart) can improve concentration, memory, and perception.

- *Romantic music* (Schubert, Schumann, Tchaikovsky, Chopin, and Liszt) can enhance sympathy, compassion, and love.

- *Impressionist music* (Debussy, Faurè, Ravel) can evoke dreamlike images and can unlock creative impulses and put you in touch with your unconscious.

- *Jazz, blues, Dixieland, soul, calypso, reggae, and dance music* can uplift and inspire, release deep joy and sadness, convey wit and irony, and affirm our common humanity.

- *Salsa, rhumba, maranga, macarena,* and other forms of South American music can set hearts racing, increase respiration, and get us moving. They can often soothe and awaken creativity at the same time.

- *Big band, pop, top 40, and country music* can engage our emotions and give a sense of well-being.

- *Rock music* (such as Elvis Presley and the Rolling Stones) can stir passions, activate movement, mask pain, release tension, or even cover up unpleasant sounds in a room. This music at times, however, can cause dissonance, stress, or pain in the body when we are not in the mood to be energetically entertained.

- *Ambient, attitudinal, or New Age music* (Steven Halpern, Brian Eno), having no dominant rhythm, can elongate a sense of space and time and can induce a state of relaxed alertness.

- *Heavy metal, punk, rap, hip-hop, and grunge* can excite the nervous system, sometimes leading to dynamic behavior and self-expression.

- *Religious and sacred music* (hymns, gospel music, and spirituals) can ground us in the moment and lead to deep peace and spiritual awareness. It can be used to help us transcend and release our pain.

Students are encouraged to select music through reflections cultivated in each category here in order to discover roles that have been assigned to each gender, through musical creations.

They listen to the selections and make a list of words used to describe women and those used to describe men in the selections. They form a circle with females in the center and males on the perimeter to discuss their lists. Only females may speak; males must only listen and make no response whatsoever. After fifteen minutes or so, they reverse the positions and roles.

After each person has had an opportunity to speak, students break into groups to discuss the creation of a collage that would express their views. Each group should have males and females as they plan their collages and decide how to represent the musical stereotypes used. Students could create one large collage, with each group contributing one section, or several smaller collages.

One member records the conclusions of the group and suggestions are made related to music as a tool for improvement in gender-related communications.

QUESTIONS CAN HELP STUDENTS RESPOND TO CHANGE

Well-developed questions can help students to respond to change and to apply their skills to problems that change brings. Improvements, such as new ways to reach higher standards, can be stifled by people who cling to their familiar turf and outdated approaches without questioning their assumptions. Because questions have long been used to motivate interest and activate thinking skills, questions can help learners appreciate the role of change. Questions are an excellent means of guiding students into lively discussions about change.

One reason that classroom cultures wither is that faculty fail to challenge old, comfortable approaches. In contrast, brain-based leaders create a climate where students' worth is determined by their willingness to learn new skills and seize new responsibilities. In other words, brain-based leaders perpetually reinvent their jobs as facilitators. The most important question in this climate is not "How well do teachers teach?" Instead, it is "How much did students learn?" Another question that comes up frequently in roundtables I attend is "How much do we need to change to improve learning so that students reach higher standards?" In these circles accountability is welcomed, key questions are asked, and people are willing to change.

Developing Questions

There are several ways to develop questions that will lead students to higher levels of thinking about almost any important concept. Good questions prime students' critical faculties. Students can also formulate their own questions, which leads them into critical reading and critical thinking abilities. How do we teach students to ask probing questions? All teachers and students can develop the art of questioning through practice and reflection. In developing questions for improving a specific learning activity, keep in mind the following points:

1. What specific thinking outcome do you want to develop?

2. How are your questions ordered? That is, which questions will build on ideas from previous questions?

3. What actions are taken or not taken to clarify vague questions? To provide appropriate clues? To extend thinking on a given topic?

4. What is the best approach to follow when students cannot answer a question? Should you wait and provide thinking time? Provide further clues? Jump in and answer the question?

5. How can you develop clear, unambiguous questions?

6. How can students develop focused questions?

It is important to determine your desired outcomes in developing questions to ask. The following guidelines can help in choosing and defining the questions you want to ask students in order to achieve higher learning:

Choosing Various Kinds of Questions

1. Open-ended questions encourage students to think beyond the evidence currently at hand.

2. Discussion questions require each student to present an oral or written answer consisting of a sentence or more in her own words. These questions are fairly easy to compose and can lead the learners into many categories of thinking.

3. Factual questions demand specific facts or memorized concepts from students.

Defining What Questions You Need

1. If you require the exact facts, ask specific, fact-finding questions.

2. If you require an examination of evidence to determine its relevance to the author's purposes and predictions, ask discussion questions.

3. If you require students to relate what they read to their own predictions, ask open-ended questions.

4. If you require confirmation, modification, extension, refinement, or rejection of the author's purposes and predictions, ask discussion questions.

Thought-Starting Questions

Earlier, we discussed a constructivist approach to learning. This approach employs a student's past knowledge and past experience. Following are several thought-provoking questions to guide this learning process.

Questions That Introduce a Lesson

1. What do you already know about . . . ?

2. Why is . . . important today?

3. Where can we find evidence that . . . is useful?

4. How is . . . used in most instances?

Questions That Reflect on Past Experience

1. How do you feel about . . . ?

2. Have you ever seen . . . in action?

3. What have you done that is most like . . . ?

4. From your perspective, how is . . . a help or hindrance?

How does today's lesson relate to your real life experiences?

Questions That Build Interest

1. What would you like to know about . . . ?

2. What do you think you will be required to know about . . . ?

3. Where can we find information about . . . ?

4. What questions do you have about . . . ?

Checklist of Questioning Techniques

Following is a sample checklist that might further help you and your learners to develop a repertoire of skillful techniques:

- Have you prepared a list of questions ahead of time? (Consider the outcomes you are looking for and the information available to students.)

- Have you worded the question so that an entire group will want to think about and consider the best answer?

- Have you asked questions to obtain facts and concepts and questions that require reasoning, reflective thinking, and exposition?

- Have you used questions daily but also used other methods of inquiry, such as tests, role-plays, projects, or mapping, to activate students' ideas?

- Do you have a clear concept of how much information students should cover in their answers? Aside from being concise and precise, did your questions lead in a specific direction toward your next learning goal?

- Have you provided thinking time for students who require reflection before they speak? Did you give clues or provide another explanation for students who don't know the answer?

- Have you incorporated humor into questions? (The most effective humor is self-directed humor. It helps students enjoy the questions and feel less threatened by the possibility of making mistakes.)

- Have the questions provided an opportunity for students to respond to other students? (Don't make question periods a ping-pong response in which every answer is sifted through the teacher's ideas. Allow several students to take turns responding to questions, and you will create a round-table question period.)

- Have you treated all students in a respectful manner, without allowing any preconceived attitudes to underestimate (or overestimate) responses? (When we refuse to play favorites, students are freed to take risks and make progress.)

- Have you questioned from the known to the unknown? (If you use a constructivist approach, questions can move learners from personal knowledge to a construction of new ideas or conclusions.)

In order to celebrate what students know, questions should be worded to help build their confidence to learn. Questions should generally be straightforward, without tricks or traps. Research shows that students learn more from encouragement than from sarcasm, from praise rather than criticism, and from positive rather than negative responses. In the most successful communities, enthusiasm and optimism replace cynicism and pessimism. This process begins with the facilitator and ends with students' higher-level learning. This brain-based approach can be learned by any who wish to improve their teaching to enhance their students' learning.

VYGOTSKY'S ZONE OF PROXIMAL DEVELOPMENT

Constructivists have suggested ways to think about learning for our students. But how do you discover the learning potentials for each child in your class at any given moment? How do you know what a child is ready to learn and on what solid foundation new knowledge can be built?

Russian psychologist and constructivist Lev Vygotsky believed we can discover these potentials in a social setting that is rich with demonstrations and challenges. He emphasized ways that the teacher or facilitator shows competency and curiosity so that students will feel comfortable doing tasks with the "expert" today and comfortable doing those same tasks alone tomorrow. In what Vygotsky called the "zone of proximal development," learners arrive at any lesson with internal stories of mastery already in place, "harvests" of success produced by prior experiences in many social settings, such as family, friends, peers, churches, and playgrounds.

Children are ready to learn much more, just not all at once. What they are prepared to learn at any specific moment lies in the zone of proximal development. Simply put, their past experiences prepare them to master new realities that are presented to them. Activities that prepare students to learn new tasks might be singing, sharing stories about a topic, dancing, or any task that would relate to the new lesson but that also reaches back and draws out prior knowledge and experiences on that topic.

A Constructivist Approach to a Science Lesson

One science teacher hoped to activate students' ideas and bring their former knowledge to their new learning tasks. She wrote the word *power* on the board and circled it. Students were to call out whatever came to their minds on this topic but to include only topics they knew something about and wanted to learn more about. The ideas were as widespread as the students' zones, as each new thought triggered another. Student ideas included the following:

force	ramps/levers/loads	earthquakes
motion	efficiency	heat/temperature
gravity	work over time	quantity
mass/weight	energy—kinetic, mechanical, electrical, potential, chemical	fossil fuels versus other sources
work		
$w = f \times d$		ethics
ability to do work	nuclear nature of volcanoes	Scientific Revolution
work = machines		Kuhn

In another science class, the students illustrated their unique interests and abilities on the topic of change. Their ideas included the following:

chemical changes	biological change	genetics
reactions	personal/social	population
electrochemistry	evolutionary	birth/reproduction

EMBRACING CHANGE USING THE MITA MODEL

Teachers who draw students into the learning process in this way discover new interest and curiosity in their learners. Students take ownership of their learning.

But if each person comes to learning with a different zone of proximal development, how can a facilitator keep track? When delivery of content is uppermost in a teacher's or leader's priorities, chances are that much of what is being taught will fall outside the zones of some learners. The result is that content will not make sense for these learners.

You do not have to provide unique learning situations for each learner on a daily basis. According to Vygotsky, when we create a social environment, students will naturally discover their unique roles. Learning becomes a social activity that can be shared with people in other cultures, with people who hold different beliefs, and with people in a variety of settings. If you provide learning opportunities within a social setting, you will be able to explore changes in interesting new ways.

In a Foundations of Education course I taught, we applied the brain-based MITA model to learning. I challenged master-level teachers to embrace change in ways described in this chapter. The motto was: Risk changes that will lead to learning and assessment improvements. In our roundtable discussions, questions flew on every issue, and barriers to change were discussed, with solutions suggested by each group.

At these teacher preparation roundtables, we looked for innovative ways that traditional university classes might change and lead to learning beyond the classroom. The groups investigated current learning theories and expressed their conclusions about how to make changes for improvements through Gardner's multiple intelligences. They negotiated assessment of their projects by adding criteria they wanted included in my evaluations of their work to the list of criteria I provided in rubrics.

Although the MITA model required huge changes for these education students, most loved the challenges we created together. We explored new methods of teaching that involved change by altering the way we structured our own class. The ripple effect of the enthusiasm generated in this group was awe inspiring. The group shed cynicism and pessimism in exchange for creative questions and suggestions for practical changes that started in our group. Rejecting complaining and negative attitudes, which tend to build similar behaviors in others, this group made the choice to achieve together new active-learning tasks for their secondary students. Because they began to believe they could be the best and because they created a vision for what this best would look like in their classes, they surpassed the grim litany of "realism" they described in their schools. Their visions of what could be had turned them into idealists, and they shared stories of huge barriers they'd overcome in their schools.

Another student suggested that we should adopt the attitude of Einstein and other change agents, who enjoyed what critics sometimes term "unrealistic" goals.

We decided to try a few new settings beyond the university to develop and share creative ideas. One time, for instance, we stepped out of the traditional university class setting and met for a day in the country. We played with new ideas pooled from our unique mix of gifts and sought many new entry points into the course content.

The most significant challenges came from teachers who had grown so enthusiastic about using their special gifts in assignments that they often worked late into the night and sometimes found too little time for their other master-level courses. Even in this highly motivated group, we found that change took time. It required a step-by-step, collaborative approach that engaged new mental approaches suggested by each person in the group.

Weekly we reflected about where we had been and where we were headed in relation to the changes we hoped to implement in schools. Most of these changes related to changing a school culture from stand-and-deliver approaches to brain-based activities that would engage secondary students as they themselves had been engaged in our circles. These educators wanted to understand the rationale for each change before embracing it with a practical tactic they could implement. In order to organize our questions and roll out plans for improvement, we highlighted the main differences between a traditional approach to learning and a brain-based MITA approach. This chart eventually became our main guide to the changes we implemented, since it showed problems on one side and suggested solutions on the other.

Table 6.1 can be useful to your roundtables as you look at lesson plans you have used and suggest changes you'd like to implement to ensure higher motivation and achievement in your students.

TABLE 6.1   Differences between Traditional and MITA Teaching Approaches

	Traditional Approach	**MITA Approach**
Lesson Plan	• Teacher predetermines facts to deliver in text or lecture. • Teacher-as-expert determines right and wrong responses. • Alternative ideas are rarely considered. • Memory aids are used. • Tests are formal and standardized.	• Learning is multimodal. • A variety of paths to knowledge are opened. • Diversity and conflict are welcomed. • Ambiguity is tolerated. • Paradox is embraced. • Interests and abilities are employed as entry points to deeper understanding.
Motivation	• Motivation is extrinsic. • Students desire higher grades or fear failure.	• Motivation is intrinsic. • Personal talents and abilities are celebrated as conduits to new knowledge.
Intelligences Activated	• Facts are memorized. • Performance is rigidly constrained. • Lessons involve minimal use of dendrites.	• Problems are solved. • New products are created. • A wide variety of intellectual approaches are employed.
Results	• Facts are forgotten over time. • Text is unrelated to students' interests and abilities. • Learning occurs in isolation. • Curriculum is unrelated to life beyond text. • Students are bored. • Learning is at lower level for the most part.	• Knowledge is more related to students' gifts and abilities. • Content is integrated into a variety of disciplines. • Group members motivate one another. • Lessons are related to community life beyond the textbook. • Further inquiry is promoted through high interest levels. • Critical thinking skills are employed.

Using the MITA/traditional comparison, we discussed how MITA at times includes qualities from the traditional side, and vice versa. We did not wish to get sidetracked in a right/wrong debate, but we wanted to experiment with solid guidelines for a strong roundtable community. We constantly asked the question "How can we promote learning beyond our classroom environment to build a roundtable community?" Our experiment was successful beyond our wildest imaginations, especially as we bonded through a common purpose.

All forty-seven of us met at my friends Art and Judy's huge estate in Georgetown on a crisp, clear Saturday morning in January. Before that day, we discussed how outdoor education and education beyond the classroom can enhance lesson plans and motivation, activate intelligences, and result in learning. Following are the questions we asked:

1. **Lesson plan**—How does outdoor education employ the students' interests and abilities as entry points to deeper understanding? We devised the following integrated activity for high school or college classes.

ACTIVITY 6.1   Walk for Fitness and Problem Solving

Outcome

A simple weekly graph of teachers' and students' walking and problem-solving progress

Discussion and Procedure

Devise a method for tracking your walks, such as using rough estimates of the distances or using a pedometer to log miles. Relate the topic you are studying to your walk in as many ways as possible. In a class hike, students pair up and discuss a question concerning their work. Students brainstorm for a variety of ways to log and record their walks.

In groups of four, the students create a poster that displays how walking influences fitness and health. They study at least one famous hiker and describe this person's walking patterns. They locate several destinations that would be similar in distance to their walking distance.

---

2. **Motivation**—In what ways can learning beyond the classroom celebrate students' talents and abilities in a genuine quest for new knowledge? We devised the following activity in which students could justify their own thinking as a motivation activity.

ACTIVITY 6.2   Justify Your Own Thinking

Outcome

A list of the series of solutions that led to a final outcome

Discussion and Procedure

Change that lasts often comes in step-by-step stages. Change is also a learned process, and its parts can be examined through reflection, so that students can use similar problem-solving strategies to create changes in their worlds beyond class. Anybody can train bright, willing students in the fundamentals of a lesson topic, but brain-based facilitation stirs up in learners integrity, judgment, energy, balance, and the drive to apply real solutions to complex problems.

In circles that involve students collaboratively, students brainstorm and list the stages of their thinking process that led them to a final solution. This reflective activity helps students "unpack" their own thought processes and apply them to the changes they hope to create. Students were motivated as their unique thinking patterns were validated. Store the completed reflections about changes students would make in their portfolios and compare them to other students' and researchers' thinking stages and processes throughout the term. In this way you can apply students' ideas and insights about change to theories about change found in their texts. To explore these issues further, engage their unique gifts and discuss their past experiences.

3. **Intelligences activated**—How does learning beyond the classroom help students solve problems, create new products, and employ a wide variety of intellectual approaches? We developed the following activity to help students find ways to implement changes to include use of their strengths.

ACTIVITY 6.3   Building Multiple Intelligence Centers

Outcome
Student-created centers for the eight ways of knowing

Discussion and Procedure
When groups build practical plans of action by brainstorming the parts, they have already taken steps to carry out those plans. This is how the brain works. Think of it as building new neuron pathways from your vision of what you hope to achieve to your progression toward achieving that target. The brain actually rewires itself to help you get to the target. In this way, you physically build new neuron pathways in your brain to achieve your improvements.

This integrated unit takes place over approximately one month. Students create a variety of centers for expressing their projects in a variety of ways. Students choose one intelligence that represents their strength. With others who enjoy similar ways of knowing, students create centers for the classroom. Each center contains several student-created activities that invite a response using one of Gardner's eight ways of knowing. Students choose the topic with the teacher; the topic comes from the unit being taught. Students create innovative banners or posters to distinguish the centers.

Students may wish to consult at times with other groups, who may be weaker in their chosen skills. Such consultation will enable student designers to create realistic activities through which others who visit the completed centers can develop their weaker skills. All students eventually will visit all centers, and in some cases, parents may visit the centers at a special presentation. Teachers participate in this activity as knowledge brokers, assistants, and facilitators. Names of those who created materials should be listed at each center. Parents can be invited either to participate in activities or to help students create the center. Some parents may enjoy helping students build their centers.

The following is a sample of the activities students did at each center:

1. **Mathematical-logical:** Students brainstorm for activities related to their topic. These include math, visual activities, problem solving, and so on.

2. **Verbal-linguistic:** Students brainstorm for activities that explore the topic through reading, writing, speaking, debating, media, and so on.

3. **Visual-spatial:** Students brainstorm for visual arts activities, geometry, and spatial recording such as graphs, diagrams, and so on.

4. **Musical-rhythmic:** Students brainstorm for activities that include vocal, sound distinctions, instrumental, cultural contributions, and so on.

5. **Bodily-kinesthetic:** Students create physical education activities, dance, coordination, role-playing, building projects, and so on.

6. **Interpersonal:** Students brainstorm for activities that involve relations with others, mutual respect, multicultural understanding, group problem solving, and so on.

7. **Intrapersonal:** Students brainstorm for activities that develop self-confidence, responsibility, self-management, ethics, and so on.

8. **Naturalistic:** Students brainstorm for links between the topic and solutions found in nature. Or they discuss and illustrate possibilities that might be supported by a naturalist.

---

4. **Results**—How does learning outside the classroom integrate a variety of disciplines? Employ critical thinking skills? Relate to life beyond the textbook? Promote high levels of interest for further inquiry?

As we met and moved in and out of one another's circles and discussed learning, we found that learning and enjoying new ideas beyond our classrooms helped us avoid being limited by fear of failure and worry about grades. We were able to build community and to connect important knowledge bases.

Change can often take place more readily outside of the familiar context, so it is often a good idea to plan innovative meeting places on a few occasions. One roundtable I facilitated met in the country, where we brought skates for use on the family's outdoor ice rink, warm winter clothing for hikes through a cave site, our adventuresome spirits for rides down the hill on a flying trapeze, and ideas to share as we sipped hot chocolate around a pot-bellied stove.

We brainstormed ideas for how we might use the MITA approach to welcome diversity, tolerate ambiguity, and embrace paradox in an evening of renewal that included members of the community. Because we shared a fantastic time together away from the classroom, we incorporated activities designed to make learning between top performers and low achievers more motivational and beneficial, and we took a few risks together to create a student-led conference that involved the parents in wonderful ways.

TEACHERS' AND LEARNERS' ROLES IN CREATING POSITIVE CHANGE

Change can be positive when it is openly discussed and understood. Teachers, students, and parents are asking questions about the basic rubrics of learning, and their collaborative answers are changing the way schools do business. Change is inevitable, and our vision for change, our collective skills, and our community resources help to define that change. In roundtables, teachers and students find the courage to avoid simply becoming swept along with changes that lack positive results.

Questions that parents, teachers, and students ask most often concern the roles of teachers, learners, power, curriculum decisions, and assessment. Ask yourself, "What is the role of the teacher?" Use the words in your answer to generate more questions. The words should correspond to the questions.

With curricular changes that transform passive listening toward active roundtable approaches to teaching and learning, new teaching strategies will begin to shift the role of teachers in secondary schools from "sage on the stage" to "guide to the side." Access to knowledge has expanded enormously, and we know far more about teaching and learning than we knew a decade ago. At the same time, shrinking budgets have reduced the number of important resources from which teachers can glean new ideas. The challenge is to draw more on the resources we have at hand—the amazing minds of all students who enter our classes.

Consider how education has changed since you attended high school, where teachers stood at the front and rows of students sat passively taking notes or responding to questions. A roundtable center, in contrast, is a place where the teacher is any person who contributes an idea on the topic, where the best ideas reside within a pool of participants' resources, and where students reach beyond themselves into the community for wisdom, experience, and partnership.

In spite of the demands and challenges, however, we must hold an image of teacher that guides our profession. In roundtable, we decide what this image of teacher will be in an ideal setting. Agreeing about what teachers should know and what abilities and attitudes they should have can lead to common standards for practice and provide critical components for high-quality teaching.

Teachers' Roles

Teacher actions for roundtable learning include the following:

1. *Serve students.* Care and commitment to students provide the cornerstone of education in a brain-based roundtable setting. Students' welfare remains at the center of all learning and assessment activities. Teachers who collaborate in interactive circles with their students express genuine sensitivity to race, gender, culture, and socioeconomic differences among their students. The goal in roundtable learning is to create productive learning environments for all students.

2. *Relate ideas about content through appropriate teaching strategies.* Teachers in roundtable act as a knowledge resource at times and model the integration of connected ideas. By modeling effective teaching strategies, they make knowledge accessible to students as well as facilitate the development of their learning. Simply put, they practice a wide variety of teaching approaches in order to address student differences.

3. *Motivate student learning.* When teachers motivate one student in a roundtable approach, they improve the quality of learning for the entire group. Each person's contribution is valued, and so each helps to improve learning for the group. Motivation may involve setting clear goals with a student and parent, conferencing to assess the students' interests and abilities in order to reshape a project, or simply asking the circle to provide ideas for an upcoming unit.

4. *Collaborate with others in the circle.* High school teachers have been taught to work alone. But if we are to meet the new challenges of learning, which include information overload and changes in technology, we must select partners and mentors for support. Roundtable learning involves colleagues, students, parents, and the community. The teacher uses information gathered in discussions to improve student learning.

5. *Commit to lifelong learning.* Teachers must become reflective and take regular inventory of their own practice. Teachers must continue to learn throughout their careers, through consistent reflection on research and the literature of the profession. In other words, teachers who are committed to roundtable will be professionals who take the lead in developing new classroom practices consistent with what we now know about learning and teaching. They will be involved in research and scholarship as well as in promoting quality practice that reflects the foregoing standards.

Learners' Roles

The roles of students in roundtable learning (see Poplin and Stone, 1992) are highlighted below:

1. *Support peers when they take risks for improvements.* Group and individual commitment to every student characterizes the roundtable setting. Each student is considered gifted, and the group's task is to uncover and celebrate each person's abilities. Students express a genuine appreciation for race, gender, culture, and socioeconomic differences among their peers. The goal of students is to help create a productive learning environment for all.

2. *Choose appropriate teaching and learning strategies to relate ideas.* Students in roundtable provide knowledge and relate the integration of connected ideas through a wide variety of resources. By choosing effective teaching and learning strategies, they contribute knowledge to other students while facilitating the development of their own learning. In roundtable, students choose teaching and learning approaches in keeping with their individual differences.

3. *Motivate independent learning.* In a roundtable approach, students motivate one another to improve the quality of learning for the entire group. Motivation may involve setting clear goals with other students and parents, conferencing to assess the common interests and abilities in order to create meaningful projects, or brainstorming within the circle to provide ideas for an upcoming unit.

4. *Collaborate with others in the circle.* High school students often work alone, which is appropriate for some learning performances. But learning partnerships are also important in most tasks if students are to understand the issues and enjoy alternative perspectives. Roundtable learning fosters collaboration with teachers, peers, parents, and the wider community. In roundtable, students use information gathered in discussions to improve individual and group learning.

5. *Commitment to lifelong learning.* Students must reflect or think about their own thinking, a process called metacognition that is encouraged throughout brain-compatible lessons suggested in this book. Rather than merely coming up with answers to a problem, students reflect on how they solved that problem and use the information to develop new strategies for solving other, related problems. The idea is that all people are always learning, and the process cannot be stopped.

FINDING RENEWAL IN ROUNDTABLE SETTINGS

Students in roundtable settings learn how to acquire and apply knowledge within community by using their unique abilities and drawing on fellow learners for additional resources. Faculty also enjoy regular personal renewal alongside their students. The following questions can help you find renewal within brain-based roundtables:

1. How are you adding to your own passion and enthusiasm for quality outcomes and adding to others' motivation as you go?

2. How have you showed that you cared what others think and do? How have you entered into many worlds beyond your own in any learning circle?

3. How have you been surprised by joy daily? How does this come across to those who choose to think and grow and change within the ebb and flow of ordinary events?

4. How do you encourage steady progress that results in growth?

5. How do you value what experiences you have lived? How do you build new experiences onto established roots in symbiotic links?

6. How are you learning to laugh at little things and at yourself in class?

7. How are you showing generosity to people and events daily in order to motivate positive interactions with you, from "deep to deep," before you make decisions to move on?

8. What positive metaphors become your lenses to live with learning, integrity, and care within images that foster your own and the group's plans for better insights?

9. How do you help the group to step out past criticism and risk dancing into new insights for your call to mastery?

10. Do you question your own performance at each day's end, by asking "Where to from here?"

Answers spring up from within and keep us moving on, into daily personal renewal and away from blaming others for what we are learning along the way. Renewal brings growth to a reflective person, and that growth is revealed in changes within entire communities. If change were easy, we would see more of it alive in secondary school communities. We'd see more college professors collaborate effectively and value their research, their students, and their colleagues. Instead, the most innovative leaders in the field will often tell you that change is difficult. Even as you create vibrant, open, collaborative brain-based cultures, with higher achievement and happier participants, prepare to experience times that are lonely whenever you initiate changes in the status quo. And prepare to experience a few risks that end in rather unexpected or disappointing results.

PRINCIPLES ABOUT CHANGE

Few would deny that change comes only with difficulty in high schools or colleges. In order to introduce a variety of innovative teaching approaches, I first had to identify my reason for making changes. Change for the sake of change can be harmful to learning. My question was "How can we create classrooms that reflect what we know about effective learning and teaching practices?" My response was to introduce Gardner's multiple intelligences theory into classrooms in a respectful and collaborative way.

It important to consider "Why does change work in some classrooms and not in others?" This is a starting point for many roundtables of faculty and students. Responses have demonstrated that the change process itself is more significant than we think. The changes described here are integrative. For this reason we are not always able to recognize what makes change work well in some settings, while similar changes result in an uphill battle in other climates. Nevertheless, there are a few common elements that can guide the work you do in roundtables to promote improvements for higher motivation and achievement.

In the process of working with teachers, students, and parents to develop the MITA model, I learned several significant principles of change. These eight may provide springboards for your own changes in high school or college, or the ideas may provide a framework for your own ideas about change.

1. *Initiate change in small increments—geographically, technologically, and conceptually.* Students and teachers need time and support in order to temper concerns with mastery of the three R's (which traditionally characterized curriculum in high schools) with skills to adapt new knowledge to contemporary challenges, such as technology in a changing society. In other words, change should more than cover the curriculum basics and do so through a variety of ways, such as the roundtable and multiple intelligences approaches.

2. *Help others by doing projects with them, by working alongside.* Teachers and students who activate one another's interests and abilities erect pillars in structures that counteract deeply ingrained, top-down teaching habits. Working together, each one brings unique responses to a common problem until the group is satisfied with the solutions chosen.

3. *Respect human dignity.* Draw on the experience and knowledge of each one in the group. When students hook new knowledge onto past ideas and past experiences, they demystify complex new ideas. In learning that begins with students' knowledge and experience, participants enjoy a role in the production of knowledge, and their unique abilities become a knowledge-producing vehicle.

4. *Achieve innovation at minimum cost by using local resources.* Often, the best resources are those closest to you. Students and teachers are nourished and energized through their shared responsibility for positive changes. Parents can also

bring specialized resources, such as the sealskin boot-sewing demonstration Olassie, an Inuit elder on Baffin Island, gave to my class.

5. *Complete all tasks with excellence and evaluate them.* Through performance-based assessment, or the direct observation and rating of student performance, evaluation becomes an ongoing process. And learning assessment provides students with many opportunities to apply knowledge to real-life situations. As a result, students are more likely to achieve excellence.

6. *Share what you have learned with others.* Ideas not shared have little power to bring about lasting changes. Students, parents, and teachers who exchange knowledge grow together. Learning becomes interactive and active. In one classroom I recently visited, a grade 10 group created collaborative projects to illustrate their learning about five countries. Students arranged displays in stalls, where bright flags and each country's emblems boldly proclaimed its place. Parents came to enjoy international food and to interact with students about research, multicultural ideas, and displays. Students engaged their parents on shared questions about each assignment they completed, and they seemed to learn more as they taught these concepts to their parents in an interactive manner. The room was charged with enthusiasm, since this student-led task gave students a place at the helm of their own learning. Displays included Gardner's eight ways of knowing. Each stall included music, dance, dining, industrial frameworks, art, historic reports, and samples of architectural designs.

7. *Create both personal and group satisfaction.* As high school teachers, students, and parents interact, they gain new appreciation and interest, not only in ideas but also in one another. Classes benefit through group satisfaction that arises from this holistic approach to knowledge.

8. *Base innovation on wisdom, not mere knowledge.* Many believe the process of lasting change is spiritual, not merely intellectual. Inuit leaders on Baffin Island emphasize that wisdom includes such distinct characteristics as kindness, humility, caring, putting others first, and building community. These characteristics are often modeled by Inuit teachers in their classes and in circles they build with students out on the land. An overall observation I made while in the Arctic is that Inuit innovation draws more on learners' beliefs and values and draws less on rigid facts from texts or memorized answers.

There have been many communities and many students that taught me the lessons highlighted in this chapter. My lessons from the Inuit and other cultural communities have provided me a starting place, just as your unique experiences will help you to build roundtable communities in changing times. The lessons I learned from Inuit teachers and students showed how the best ideas often come when we step beyond familiar settings. In my case, those settings took me into lessons that changed the way I approached learning and teaching. While your experiences may differ, you can cull them for equally tangible responses to the problems of change in secondary and university cultures.

This collaborative culture already existed in many small northern communities, and when I began instructing in a two-year teacher education program, I reaped the benefits of dynamic community interaction. I was involved in a partnership between Arctic College and McGill University, a program established to help certify preservice Inuit teachers. Two other instructors and I rotated among the three Baffin communities—Igloolik, Arctic Bay, and Pangnirtung—over a two-year period. During this time, we frequently encountered a genial and collaborative atmosphere, especially among teachers and other community members. This chapter represents a tribute to deep lessons I learned from Inuit friends, lessons I translated into the concept of roundtable learning approaches that helped me and my students to resolve problems that change threw my way.

Frequently, changes that result from my work with other cultures come after I leave the communities and appear in times of thought, risk taking, or collaborative problem solving. Whenever we face changes, we are challenged to reflect on places we stood in the past, reasons why change has occurred, and strategies, if any, that we should use differently in the future. Insights and practical approaches highlighted in this chapter represent not only my own reflections over thirty years in the teaching profession, but also conclusions drawn from studying theory with a mind to converting the best ideas into doable practices and tactics that improve learning outcomes for more students.

This chapter integrates not only the approaches I learned in Inuit communities but also represents all I have been taught by scholars and students of many cultures who showed me the treasures hidden in a field in which I have spent a lifetime of adventures. Within the framework of a fireside chat for roundtable interaction, you can find approaches that will build on others' backgrounds, on current learning and assessment theories, and on new insights about how teachers and students can capitalize on their mental capabilities.

THE IMPORTANCE OF SLEEP ON LEARNING

Whenever faculty and students consider the impact of the human brain on learning and explore ways to improve their roundtables in brain-friendly ways, students benefit. In brain-compatible classes, students explore issues that allow them to optimize their mental capabilities. For example, few students are aware of the negative impact that lack of sleep brings. Sharing a few facts may provide huge advantages to sleep-deprived youth.

You will feel groggy if you awaken your brain in the middle of one of its sleep cycles and rhythmic patterns, which last for 90 minutes. Patterns of sleep for the normal brain generally progress through three 30-minute sessions. Complete cycles tend to last 1 hour and 30 minutes, and you don't do well when they are broken or interrupted. The sleep cycle follows this pattern:

- In the first 30 minutes, you sleep rather lightly.

- In the second 30 minutes during REM (rapid eye movement) sleep, your brain restores levels of oxygen to the cornea while you dream.

- In the third 30-minute phase, you move back into a lighter sleep. You will shorten your REM stage if you eat heavily, drink before bedtime, or take some medications.

We can help our students to enhance their wake-up time by sharing a few brain-based facts about how sleep impacts the brain. It does not require a degree in neuroscience to begin to share secrets that help students find more success at school. You can start by simply letting them know they can get more from their brains if they follow a few tips related to sleep and then adding a few suggestions, such as the following.

- Plan your sleep in 90-minute chunks, and you'll feel better when you wake up.

- Set your alarm for 20 minutes earlier than you normally awake.

- Sleep in a darkened room, and you'll help your brain release enough melatonin, a hormone that helps your brain to get the rest it needs.

You'll be surprised at the interest stirred up in students when they encounter these simple yet helpful tips. Invite students to test the ideas and to report back on their discoveries. Some students, as well as some faculty, will also delve deeper into neuroscience research and come back to the roundtables with further details. This can be seen in the response of one student, who proudly told the group of his discoveries after a brain-based discussion that tempted him to test the ideas himself.

> Have you noticed that when you sleep for the same amount of time each night, you no longer need the alarm, since your brain has its own built-in alarm once it learns your patterns?

In the same way, students can be helped to train their brains for higher performance, simply by seeing the interrelation between their sleep habits and their learning outcomes.

Just as change comes from collaborative thinking and shared problem solving, so brain-based results are often tested in these circles. Then behavioral changes that result from a change in thinking can be accomplished to increase students' higher learning.

CHAPTER 7

Faculty Roundtables— Putting It All Together

I have no special talents. I am only passionately curious.

Albert Einstein

Curiosity motivates faculty circles, and multiple intelligences fuel a group's movement toward more success at school. Tom Hoerr (2000), director at St. Louis's New City School, is an internationally respected leader in faculty roundtables that encourage excellence through Gardner's multiple intelligences theory.

Dr. Hoerr inspires faculty, parents, and students to help bring about significant and lasting change that benefits the entire community. Especially compelling is his love for diversity, multiculturalism, and his school's excellent record for surpassing state standards. I have been deeply inspired by his life work and especially by Tom's celebration of people's gifts.

Roundtables at Tom's school show the delicate balance between support and challenge, between theory and best practices. He provides concrete lessons that draw on students' strengths and engage the entire community in learning adventures. New City School's interactive learning Website is http://www.newcity school.org/home.html. The school regularly hosts faculty from across the United States and around the world. Educators want to learn from other successful leaders and especially from those who facilitate different voices, as Tom does with amazing results.

Achieving excellence is a process for Tom Hoerr, who makes it abundantly clear that the effort to use brain-based and multiple intelligences ideas effectively must remain on the agenda. Impressive progress has been made at New City School because of sustained determination to improve. We can improve schools significantly, but only if we take the long view and do not settle for patchwork, Tom suggests, and this approach differs from the one-shot workshop or the latest theoretical methods offered one at a time to busy teachers. Excellence starts at Tom's school with interest and is sustained by support and persistence. If you'd like to see the MITA recommendations from this book in action, you'll find salient ideas in Tom's circles that will work well in your own.

NOT SO MUCH TALENT AS CURIOSITY

Curiosity is the handmaiden of great ideas in secondary and college classrooms. The key is to spark and sustain curiosity in faculty and students.

Freire (2000) teaches that when faculty bring together theory and practice in meaningful ways, they show students possible dreams suddenly available to them. Progress comes whenever faculty reflect on new possibilities to include their students' past experiences, increase their present possibilities, and enhance future successes. The best teachers accomplish impressive goals through investigating current learning theories and then applying classroom practices related to learning theory and brain-based insights.

This strategy works well but requires persistence and determination and will rarely come from attending one or two professional development sessions. The student-centered tasks offered here are launching pads to spark and sustain curiosity in faculty and students.

It is impossible to benefit from MITA brain-based practices in this book without reflecting on where one is now and finding a noble vision to attain. This chapter illustrates a few strategies for faculty roundtables that are formed to envision and communicate innovative ideas in a vibrant and ongoing circle of curiosity building. Only then can brain-based theories and practices transform inquisitiveness into possibilities for success in a new millennium. This chapter suggests roundtable approaches for faculty to create and share ongoing curriculum ideas that solve real-world problems and reach across cultures to engage more students.

As Einstein's statement at the beginning of this chapter indicates, successful learning results depend more on a person's curiosity than on any talents that person might possess. Brain-based tactics combine theory and practical applications for visible results, even when we cannot see around the distant corner of pathways that lead to change.

COLLABORATION FOR CLEAR OBJECTIVES IN CHANGING TIMES

When Toto said to Dorothy in *The Wizard of Oz,* "I've a feeling we're not in Kansas anymore," he spoke for the best upper-level classrooms. The lay of the land has changed. The natives are different. This changing face of the curriculum creates similar shifts in expectations, as, for example:

- Past realities of nationalism yield today to a global perspective.

- Anglo-Americans are no longer a majority in North America.

- Hierarchical systems of control block learning relationships.

Benchmarks of this "new land" include authenticity, community, focus on the arts, and diversity. In addition to this changed landscape, emerging facts about how brains learn best will shape our new journeys toward these goals.

Given traditional constraints of upper-level education, more and more faculty who refuse to "stand and deliver" are using clear performance objectives to engage learning differences among students and build their curiosity. Performance objectives add the structure roundtables need to stay on target with complex topics. Rather than lectures, roundtable lessons are designed to address state standards by actively engaging students' brains. These explorations consist of student performances based on using many intelligences. Each objective begins with "The learner will . . . " (or TLW . . .) as a reminder that it is not so much about what teachers do in class, but what students perform. For example:

- TLW distinguish between _____, using 2 original documents.

- TLW conduct a survey to determine _____, when technology _____.

- TLW write a business proposal for a new marketing technology for peers.

When you integrate insights you may already have about performance objectives and act on even one mental fitness tactic, you begin to see how what you enjoy and do well is often enhanced by adding new dimensions. For example, we've often heard that to substitute unclear words such as *know, understand, analyze, appreciate,* or *realize* for words such as *state, demonstrate, list, describe, memorize,* or *compute,* we set visible expectations. Now we know why. Students who use more spatial intelligence will visualize in new ways that build pathways from their brains to their performances. These are not necessarily learning and assessment tasks but often indicate the nature of tasks or performance. For instance, in considering an objective, you will note the performance possibilities but will not see how this performance takes place. Will students write, speak, or demonstrate responses? One cannot tell by objectives alone, and eventually tasks are created to enable students to reach their stated objectives.

In other words, to create strong, well-stated objectives is to pave a clear direction for an active lesson plan in which students explore ideas and express them in ways that ensure understanding of the content. Students' explorations that result in higher achievement comes from careful planning in faculty roundtables.

It is often advisable to identify one or two significant learning objectives for each lesson. Some faculty begin a new unit with all objectives listed and then limit each lesson to one or two of these objectives to be accomplished within a class session. The key is clarity and specificity. Foggy objectives result in a poor grasp of content, poor participation, and classroom management problems. Time spent on creating good learning objectives is often timed saved in reteaching content. Creating objectives in each intellectual domain to solve one key content question might include the lesson objectives highlighted in the following section.

Objectives for Multiple Intelligences Lessons

Faculty roundtables work well for sharing ideas in process. While one person lists a few planned objectives, others spark eclectic additions for lessons shared. Here are examples one group created to tap into students' multiple intelligences.

Verbal-Linguistic Demonstration

- TLW list at least five major characteristics of _____ that include more diverse student groups.

- TLW create and edit a 500-word story to illustrate relationships between _____ and underrepresented groups.

Logical-Mathematical Demonstration

- TLW outline and explain the development of _____ from birth to maturity

- TLW graph barriers to _____ for underrepresented students.

Visual-Spatial Demonstration

- TLW illustrate a story to show the _____ patterns of another culture.

- TLW create a poster to guide improved _____ for diverse student groups.

Bodily-Kinesthetic Demonstration

- TLW perform a dance to illustrate _____ and lifestyles.

- TLW pantomime three typical _____ opportunities for a physical education class.

Musical-Rhythmic Demonstration

- TLW compose or illustrate music to describe _____'s influence in the arts.

- TLW identify how music influences _____ for youth.

Interpersonal Demonstration

- TLW interview three peers to determine their experiences with integrated _____.

- TLW explain how _____ impacts human friendships.

Intrapersonal Demonstration

- TLW create a journal with ten entries about personal perspectives on _____ and learning.

- TLW describe personal strengths and weaknesses in _____.

Naturalistic Demonstration

- TLW compare and contrast how naturalistic learning impacts the learner and another country's secondary school students.

- TLW show how nature provides opportunities for learning _____.

There are many options available to faculty who work together for objectives, options that remain hidden to those who work in isolation.

This chapter offers practical guidelines for collegial roundtables that teachers tell us they need. Strong, well-stated objectives start in faculty circles and lead to clear directions for student-centered learning tasks. Foggy objectives, on the other hand result in a poor grasp of where you or your students are headed. Figure 7.1 provides a checklist of critical inquiries for developing good learning objectives together or critiquing another's objectives.

As illustrated in Figure 7.1, brain-based approaches to learning objectives involve interactions with text, relationship building with others, and brainstorm-

FIGURE 7.1 Learning (or Performance) Objectives Checklist

While you may choose a variety of styles to express your performance objectives, several critical elements typically characterize clear learning objectives:

Inquiries for Good Learning Objectives

1. Are objectives measurable (that is, can you see students' performances)? _____
2. Do objectives state observable learner performances? _____
3. Do objectives outline conditions under which behaviors occur? _____
4. Are objectives stated with prescribed learner performances in mind? _____
5. Are objectives written with an action verb such as *list, compare, illustrate*? _____
6. Do objectives describe minimum expectations for all students? _____
7. Are objectives stated in as few words as possible? _____
8. Do objectives begin with "The learner will . . . " (TLW)? _____
9. Are objectives listed as brief bullets? _____
10. Does each objective describe one performance only? _____
11. Does each lesson plan use one, two, or three well-stated objectives? _____
12. Will objectives be followed by specific, appropriate assessment activities? _____

Example of Specific Performance Objectives That Include Conditions

Following is a guide to creating clear objectives:

- TLW compare a school day in Brazil and a typical day in Peru, using 2 original documents.
- TLW conduct a survey to determine how 10 Brazilian senior students describe math.
- TLW select one Spanish poem to create a tableau for the class, involving 3 peers.
- TLW write a business proposal for a Brazilian marketing enterprise for American teens.

Tips for Objectives

Activities are *not objectives* but are excellent vehicles to reach your objectives in a brain-compatible environment. Activities with rubrics are also used to evaluate your objectives. In performance objectives, substitute words such as *know, understand, analyze, appreciate,* or *realize* for words such as *state, demonstrate, list, describe, memorize,* or *compute.*

Note: "The learner will . . . " (TLW) prefixes each statement.

ing with students. Faculty help one another by asking of each other's insights, "What specific tasks will students be expected to perform in order to demonstrate each particular skill or concept taught?" Responses to this question will provide quality goals. In some cases, faculty may wish to combine their objectives and create an integrated unit on one topic. In other cases, faculty will simply add a wealth of ideas to help one person develop a topic. In one meeting, for instance, the theme *light* was chosen. The unit question asked was "How does light impact humanity?" Performance objectives listed for this theme included a number of intellectual domains:

- TLW compare and contrast light and darkness in the novel *Light a Single Candle.*

- TLW illustrate the position of images, rays, lines, and angles in mirrors.

- TLW describe the human eye and its dependency on light.

- TLW demonstrate solar power in machinery and photosynthesis.

- TLW identify five ways that light obeys mathematical laws.

- TLW listen to and distinguish between light and heavy music.

Collaborative meetings work well when a specific objective is selected and the group brainstorms to add tasks for student-centered investigations to explore that objective. One group selected this objective: TLW compare and contrast light and darkness in the novel *Light a Single Candle.*

Figure 7.2 illustrates learning tasks that address this performance objective and at the same time engage students' multiple ways of knowing and expressing knowledge.

When faculty roundtables fail to achieve their goals, participants tend to drop off. Renewal takes time and commitment as well as careful facilitation. At the MITA Renewal Center, we have found that some groups tend to ramble and, as a result, fewer of their goals are met and meetings dragged on too long. Faculty began to stay away, and some expressed resentment that too much time was taken from their evening plans. Others had to dash off to coach volleyball or attend committee meetings before they concluded each roundtable session. Finally one faculty member agreed to keep the group on task, and another outlined a brief

FIGURE 7.2 Comparing and Contrasting MITA Activities

- *Verbal-linguistic* activities involve the capacity to use language effectively to express light and dark similarities and differences within the novel. Poetry might be used here or speeches delivered or debates orchestrated to consider the issues.

- *Mathematical-logical* activities involve the underlying principles of light and dark systems. Students might investigate as a scientist or logician would. Or they might express their ideas through manipulation of numbers, quantities, and operations.

- *Visual-spatial* activities involve the ability to explore and represent light and darkness as a sailor or airplane pilot might in navigating. They also involve artistic expressions or a graphic mapping of ideas and concepts.

- *Bodily-kinesthetic* activities involve the use of one's whole body or part of the body to express content learned. Light and dark problems might be solved through use of hands, fingers, arms, and legs to make something or put on a production as an athlete, performing artist, or dancer might.

- *Musical-rhythmic* activities involve listening to musical patterns, recognizing beats or rhythms, remembering chords, or manipulating notes.

- *Interpersonal* activities involve learning and teaching relationships with other people related to light and dark issues. Using the strengths of each member of a small group, one might show how each person's expressed limitations about the topic can be overcome.

- *Intrapersonal* activities involve personal reflections and questions about the topic as it relates to oneself. A person's worldview and prior knowledge might be expressed here as well as personal insights, critical questions, or personal humanistic issues.

- *Naturalistic* activities involve discrimination of light and dark features found within one's natural environment. Features here might include those of concern to farmers, botanists, chefs, or archaeologists.

agenda for each meeting. In this way, the group agreed on shared goals and outcomes before discussing implementation of any new ideas for their classes.

Even with this reduction of time, a few faculty protested that collaboration was taking up their time for teaching and assessing. Many protested excessive pressures and demands. We took one full meeting to brainstorm the pros and cons of meeting every second week, and in the end the group decided to stick with the circle for another year.

Faculty who collaborate with others, regardless of academic discipline, unleash enormous creativity and motivation to share ideas and ask questions. This process leads to clearer goals because we question meanings as others put ideas forward. Through ideas generated in a roundtable approach, we learn not only to articulate well but also to listen well, a key tool that helps students set their own clear goals. This tool helps to ensure lifelong learning. When we know exactly where we are headed, we are more likely to arrive there successfully. For instance, if you show students a digital video similar to the one they will be creating, they will go after their goal with more confidence. They can show their results to others to keep innovative ideas alive. As faculty share ideas, lesson dimensions plunge deeper than any one person's plans or strengths. Figures 7.3, 7.4, 7.5 and 7.6 are outlines of units in English, social studies, science, and mathematics that follow a brain-based MITA approach. These ideas may spark insights for your roundtable sessions.

FIGURE 7.3   English Unit Using a MITA Brain-Based Approach

Area: English   **Unit theme:** Neruda's poetry and your poetry.
Unit question: How might you see life through Neruda's eyes?

Lesson Number	Lesson Theme	Lesson Questions	Performance Objectives
1	Odes in our lives	How might Neruda write an ode about your life?	• Create 10 flashcards to teach odes to class. • Describe one Neruda ode that best describes you.
2	Nature in poetry	How does Neruda show nature to your 5 senses?	• Walk in woods to collect artifacts you enjoy. • Create a chart to show your artifacts and Neruda's to your 5 senses.
3	Poetry and peace	How can poetry promote peace as Neruda's did?	• Support Neruda's position on peace. • Uncover 3 areas of your life where peace helped you.
4	Neruda's house and yours	How does your dream home compare to La Sabastiana?	• Construct your dream home. • Compare your dream home to La Sabastiana.
5	*Il Postina*	How can poetry help a lonely postman find love?	• Watch and discuss *Il Postina*. • Write a poem to teach the postman about love.
6	Questions and answers	How would you reword and answer 5 Neruda questions?	• Select music for 5 of Neruda's questions. • Create 5 questions on similar topics in your life.
7	Revise your poem	How might Neruda revise your poem to publish it?	• Create a checklist to revise your writing. • Publish your writing in class poetry collection.

FIGURE 7.4   Social Studies Unit Using a MITA Brain-Based Approach

Area: Social studies   **Unit theme:** World cultures and our technology
Unit question: How has technology changed our culture?

Lesson Number	Lesson Theme	Lesson Questions	Performance Objectives
1	Our culture and technology	Which technologies most shaped our culture?	• Identify 5 forms of technology that most changed our culture. • Trace these 5 across your parents' lifetime.
2	Technology in another country	How is technology changing different countries?	• Demonstrate technology's role in a different country. • Compare technology in your own and one foreign country.
3	Early technology	What happened in the beginning?	• Recreate a model of one early technological advance. • Show advantages and disadvantages of your model.
4	Problems and technology solutions	What problem was solved by technology?	• List one problem solved through technology. • Illustrate solutions that come through technology.
5	Technology and my money	How has technology affected your parents' budget and yours?	• Role-play one impact technology brought to economic growth. • Map relationship between technology and financial growth over time.
6	Problems with technology	What problems has technology brought to you?	• Create music to identify one technology problem. • Illustrate your problem and suggest solutions.
7	Museum of cultures through technology	How can you showcase our key technologies and problems?	• Identify problems and possibilities of one technology over 100 years. • Create a plan to decrease problems and increase possibilities.

Once objectives are established, the group is ready to create multiple-intelligences tasks that will enable students to explore these objectives. In order to address Gardner's multiple ways of knowing a unit topic, a goal-setting heuristic similar to the one in Figure 7.7 might be especially useful to encourage experts and students to explore topics together. This organizational design can guide you on creative paths toward successful outcomes for more students. Figure 7.8 provides a chart for recording your own objectives.

RENEWAL IN EDUCATION

When you develop a support circle that opens access roads rather than offers recipes, you have begun to cultivate a brain-compatible community. You begin with innovative theoretical ideas that people already have and tether these familiar concepts to practical applications that foster students' motivation to understand and apply new ideas.

FIGURE 7.5   Science Unit Using a MITA Brain-Based Approach

Area: Science   **Unit theme:** Water quality in rivers by your home and beyond
Unit question: What is in water that we and animals drink?

Lesson Number	Lesson Theme	Lesson Questions	Performance Objectives
1	Quality of river water near your home	What lives in a river near your home?	• Identify the river nearest your home. • Share information about your river's water quality.
2	Visit a river near school	How would scientists gather and record water quality in your river?	• Record data on the class Website. • Compare your data with 2 peer reports.
3	An expert speaks about rivers	What can we learn about rivers from an expert?	• Suggest one expert to invite to class. • Create 3 good questions to ask the expert.
4	E-mail river data to another student	How does your data compare to another student's river quality?	• Exchange 5 e-mails about water quality with another student. • Compare data differences with your e-mail partner.
5	Your rivers and your grandparents'	How have waters changed over 100 years?	• Interview a senior concerning river water quality. • Research and present changes in rivers over time.
6	Rivers and your money	What do rivers have to do with your parents' budget?	• Track connections between rivers and the economy. • Create and keep a budget for river research.
7	Plan a river day	How can a river add quality to your life?	• Plan a canoe trip along a river. • Compare flora and fauna along your river bank as you paddle.

FIGURE 7.6   Mathematics Unit Using a MITA Brain-Based Approach

Area: Mathematics   **Unit theme:** How graphs and wars affect your life
Unit question: How could graphs make you win or lose a war?

Lesson Number	Lesson Theme	Lesson Questions	Performance Objectives
1	How graphs and war relate	How could a graph help you to win a war?	• Compare 3 graphs used to describe war. • Brainstorm uses for each graph for a specific war.
2	Graph types	Which graphs could you use?	• Construct 4 graphs without paper or pencil. • Create a poster story of graph's uses in war.
3	Graphs from both sides	How could I use different graphs from my enemies?	• Show a graph that emphasizes a war won. • Graph the same issues from a defeated soldier's view.
4	Computer aids	How do computer specialists create graphs?	• Contact and interview a computer specialist. • Design a computer graph to promote peace.
5	Graphs for your story	How could you tell your story best in a graph?	• Identify one area of your life to graph. • Create an overhead graph to show your story.
6	Graph accuracy	How accurate is accurate for graphs?	• Compare picture and bar graphs for accuracy. • Create a study sheet to ensure graph accuracy.
7	Defending graphs	How would you defend your graph to experts?	• Use graphs in a debate on war. • Compose a song or poem to enhance your graph's message.

FIGURE 7.7 Goal Setting: A Student-Peer-Teacher Process

Using this chart, students, peers, and teachers reflect together on progress observed in each of Gardner's eight intellectual domains.

How did you use each (or some) of these intelligences to set your goal?

Intrapersonal: Self-confidence, responsibility, self-management, ethics, etc.

Interpersonal: Relationship with others, respect, multicultural understanding, solving problems together, etc.

Verbal-linguistic: Reading, writing, speaking, media, word puzzles, debates, etc.

Mathematical-logical: Numbers, visual, problem solving, sequences, etc.

Visual-spatial: Visual arts, geometry, spatial reasoning, graphics, maps, etc.

Bodily-kinesthetic: Building, dance, coordination, movement, etc.

Musical-rhythmic: Vocal, instrumental, compositions, cultural sounds valued, etc.

Naturalistic: Environmental concerns brought into topics, labeling, etc.

The appendix at the end of this chapter provides practical examples for lessons in English, social studies, math, and science as well as suggestions for additional lesson topics and forms you and your students can use in lesson planning and assessment. In addition, curriculum samples in other disciplines and suggestions for many other topics are posted and updated on a roundtable Website at www.mitaleadership.com.

Renewal at the upper levels is not easy. After a lifetime in secondary and college education renewal circles, I have observed that effective faculty often

FIGURE 7.8   Chart for Adding Your Own Performance Objectives

Area: _____   Unit theme: _____

Unit question: _____

Lesson Number	Lesson Theme	Lesson Questions	Performance Objectives
1			
2			
3			
4			
5			
6			
7			

"ride the bus while pushing the bus at the same time." While innovative faculty rarely shout "Out with the old and in with the new," neither do they stand and deliver lectures or practice sheets while students endure classes unrelated to their past experiences or undirected to their future careers. Support circles look at problems with a resolution in mind and for the benefit of students at every achievement level. Redesigning high schools will open new windows into college-level learning for more students, but it is rarely easy to create cultural change.

BEYOND BOREDOM TO JOY OF LEARNING

In 2000, UCLA's Higher Education Research Institute (2000) surveyed more than 260,000 full-time college freshmen who reported boredom, drudgery, and disengagement in senior high school classes. Forty percent reported frequent boredom, nearly twice that of students' reports in 1985. Similar reports come from dropouts who increasingly abandon high school programs for other pursuits.

In a circle of support, faculty regain the sheer joy and curiosity of learning something new, and this is passed on to students. Instead of suggesting more discipline for addressing students' boredom and restless behavior, roundtables improve classroom management by introducing fresh approaches to these recurrent problems. Engage students' interests and abilities as tools for learning, Alfred Whitehead (1959) suggested, and boredom will be replaced with passion for the topic. Roundtables bring lightness and laughter that a fireside chat might add and can thus link joy and learning.

The many signs of boredom and disinterest in today's classrooms point to one missing ingredient identified by Whitehead (1959)—romance. In his rhythm of education model, Whitehead identified romance as the first impetus for all successful learning. Brain-friendly lessons can instill a fresh love for learning, a joy that comes from using faculty and students' mental capabilities more fully.

Few faculty disagree that learning, which is so delightfully natural to a child, can also excite their older students. Yet where are sparks of vitality to help us understand truth and paint its colors onto everyday tasks in high school and college classes? Where is the life that fuels unique gifts in any genius and motivates students to learn simply for the sheer joy of knowing?

Roundtable creations attempt to restore some of the wonder and romance for learning any new topic. When faculty work with others who seek innovative approaches, they plan together and ask one another, "How will that look in a classroom?" Through interactions at faculty roundtables, topics such as poetry, or river quality, or cultural differences are raised, and new approaches to learning these areas are discussed. One school I worked at started a faculty support circle to create connections between curriculum and knowledge already present in students' minds. Several teachers who taught the same students shared ideas for a thematic series in which each of four disciplines were covered and assessed.

As fellow learners, faculty also inquire and explore new content with a sense of wonder, and learning comes alive and motivates deeper understanding within supportive circles. As a result, teacher tools are developed for the integration of new kinds of learning and students' test scores rise.

INTEGRATION HELPS STUDENTS TO MAKE CONNECTIONS

Susan Kovalik (1994), Eric Jensen (1998), and Heidi Jacobs (1989), who teach with the brain in mind, show how the brain elicits patterns to make more meaningful contexts when students integrate as they learn. Because of this, more and more teachers integrate educational practices with current brain theory. The key is to provide an environment in which students can make meaning from their surroundings where the practices presented in this book are common.

Integrated connections, as natural to our minds as water to ducks, are fostered through two-footed questions that frame the roundtable lessons illustrated here as one of many paths toward renewal. Integration at its best is often unruly and at first may appear to lack design. Perhaps that is because we separate secondary disciplines; theory is isolated from practice, and teaching remains distant from action research projects.

Yet the human mind is already wired to seek meaningful relationships and to integrate facts in order to solve meaningful real-world problems related to valued topics. As teachers provide the stimuli and give guidance, students will begin to make their own deeper meanings out of the stimuli offered. Regular faculty interactions in roundtable settings create meaningful environments whereby students are inspired.

Emerson (1992) emphasized our mind's natural proclivity for integration:

> To the young mind everything is individual, stands by itself. By and by, it finds how to join two things and see in them one nature; then three, then three thousand . . . discovering roots running underground whereby contrary and remote things cohere and flower out from one stem. . . . The astronomer discovers that geometry, a pure abstraction of the human mind, is the measure of planetary motion. The chemist finds proportions and intelligible method throughout the matter; and science is nothing but the finding of analogy, identity, in the most remote parts.

Even those faculty who meet regularly to plan together may differ about which aspects of their content to integrate and with whom to collaborate. In the best schools, integrative designs exist in varying degrees. Brain-based lessons share several integrative components, which are affirmed in learning theories and also in brain research.

Two-Footed Questions Aid Integration

In my own work, I found that certain questions help to integrate facts and experiences as well as build curiosity among students. For years I could not figure out why some faculty could ask questions that stir a sense of interest so that students can react to one another as they explore complex ideas, while other faculty seem to get little or no reaction from their students.

After years of talking with students and working with faculty, I came to realize that some questions reach into students' lives and also into the depths of content. I have termed these *two-footed questions,* because they link to students and to the content to be learned. One foot steps into students' interests and abilities that will integrate with their answers or solutions. The other foot steps into the depths of new insights, ideas, or facts to be understood.

In the past few years, the two-footed question has become so popular with people I work with in several countries that these questions now play a key role in all MITA brain-based lessons. Meaningful questions also help students and faculty relate to one another as collaborative learners. If you want to know what interests a student, ask, "What would you do today if you had all the resources you need?" Apply two-footed questions to the most difficult topics you teach, and you will be amazed at how students' interest rises. Asking secondary or college students "How does this topic relate to you, and why should you care?" will help them integrate the topic with their personal goals. Whenever I work with faculty I ask two-footed questions such as "What would it take in your teaching to inspire yourself and others?" This question always leads to a wonderful discussion in which people find new supports and new answers in collaboration with others in their community.

Effective support circles do not legislate how to question, integrate, or reflect, but rather suggest practical guides and examples for accomplishing the curriculum emphasis. Faculty act as knowledge brokers to help students integrate knowledge in ways that best suit unique learning goals. When you partner with faculty as you create brain-compatible lessons, you both teach and learn from one another in order to build a cache of quality learning and assessment practices.

Integrating Ideas with Reality

In your faculty group, you can ask, "How can we develop classes that help more students prepare themselves academically for the information age we live in? Some might suggest demanding more self-discipline from students. In brain-friendly classes, students gain self-discipline by discovering personal passion for topics investigated at school. Faculty know that passion can be discovered together with students as they address core content areas with students and relate probing content questions to their real-world issues.

This requires a certain risk taking. It also requires an ability to "glance back and gaze forward." In this way, faculty can present new opportunities as they construct lesson plans together in order to connect excellence and equity to students' past experiences and future hopes. This process of relating ideas to reality through engaging people strengths is a key to renewal for any school, and the process often begins with small faculty roundtables. The traditional curriculum approach has created pathways too narrow to sustain lasting reform. Forward-looking faculty recognize the need to search out more inclusive designs that provide successful learning approaches. It often helps to look back to consider where traditional lessons came from and discuss how to keep what works well and how to change the rest.

BUILDING EFFECTIVE ROUNDTABLES

Roundtable support groups can take various formations. In launching your first roundtable, your group might prefer to discuss the key questions that guided their classes that week. If you start with two-footed questions, participants' interest will be captured as they also explore the content to be covered. In a second meeting your group might list and share their learning objectives. In this way, the group explores targets for a specific topic. In the third meeting, your group could create rubrics together for getting quality results for a lesson. At the next meeting, the group may map out, in specific terms, the multiple intelligence tasks that move students to actively explore the knowledge. You can use the many roundtable tasks offered in this book to develop successful teaching and learning, but it is wise to not try to change too much too soon. Faculty who achieve the best results pick one small place to start.

Effective roundtables sometimes start with a discussion of common complaints. In one roundtable I attended, teachers felt that their secondary school had lapsed into a similar crisis today as secondary schools in America after Russia launched *Sputnik*. The history teachers shared how American status in world academic assessment ratings appeared to be threatened. "Do you see any comparisons?" they challenged. The topic fired hot debates about how universities were responsible for diminished curriculum. Secondary faculty felt they were accused of not teaching basic academic knowledge, especially in math and sciences literacies (see Lucas, 1996).

Another history teacher described the 30-year downward trend in academic achievement scores and the apparent disintegration of the traditional canon that set a course for ongoing reform after *Sputnik.* These comments sparked questions about whether today's secondary classrooms felt any of these reform benefits.

We shared ideas about how the formation of councils for basic education helped define reform movements at that time (see Goodlad, 1997) and compared these councils with the roundtable started in their school. After much discussion, the faculty concluded that reform then placed an emphasis on preparing students for a liberal undergraduate education that aimed to prepare them for the intelligent life described by educators such as Cornel Hamm (1989). The biggest question at that session was "Had this goal worked?" I am not sure we left the circle with any watertight answers, but that discussion hooked people's imaginations about what a school that worked together could do to improve learning and teaching.

During another roundtable session, faculty considered this question, "Has secondary education learning and teaching sacrificed intellectual opportunities for many students in its quest for excellence?" (see Burgess, 1984). They also asked, "Has a zest for scientific and technological renewal squeezed out the possible development of additional intelligences in high school classes?" A society in moral crisis requires reflective as well as math and science curriculum (Ravitch, 1983); when that reflection starts with higher performance in mind, an entire community benefits. We now know that whenever students engage more of their brain capacity to solve complex problems, high school learning scores soar (Gardner, 1991).

Each roundtable group will differ about where it should start. I have found that it is best to start with a topic of interest to faculty in any circle and then brainstorm about how to structure the meetings when the group is ready to begin building curriculum together. One springboard into renewal roundtables for your group is to list expectations in flexible and relevant ways that enable diverse students to achieve (Perkinson, 1987). The key is to find solutions that work. Rather than disregard traditional values of discipline and hard work, for example, look for a new approach that will help all students perform more intellectual tasks or solve complex life problems. Pilot the approach and share results at the next gathering.

Remember to look for and create tools that challenge differences among students. Nurturance of diverse students need not precipitate neglect of values, rigor, or content (Bunting, 1987). The converse is also true. Care and respect often generate increased effort from students (Weber, 2000). Strict and yet clear academic standards, when accompanied by genuine inclusion, increase the opportunities for many underrepresented students to succeed. If faculty roundtables infuse time, energy, and resources into creating a curriculum that accommodates more student differences to reach higher goals, students' success is guaranteed in almost every instance, even in lower-performing schools.

After over 30 years in this work, I've discovered that whenever we wait for ideal circumstances to surface before we launch renewal initiatives, we often wait in vain. When the MITA Renewal Center was launched in New York, few resources existed initially, and some scholars asked, "Why bother?" Secondary schools, some told us, are locked in the past, and history shows that secondary faculty rarely change or renew. Others told us that school boards care about everything but students' benefits. One trustee reported that board meetings usually concentrate more on faculty conditions than on learning possibilities for students.

At the MITA Renewal Center, we don't believe that all is gloom. We stake our future on facts that show improvement is already well under way in some secondary and college classes.

ONLINE ROUNDTABLES: BUILD ON WHAT YOU KNOW

After discussions with hundreds of teachers and administrators who recognize the problems and work for improvements, we are encouraged with recent international renewal initiatives in Chile, Mexico, and Australia and with renewal efforts in our local Rochester, New York, area. This initiative includes recent online developments that allow teachers and students to chart new waters in brain-based learning. Currently, I teach secondary and university faculty online and lead professional development sessions in which faculty begin their own roundtables. Recently, I have begun brain-based certification programs for faculty, which conclude with an evening of their students teaching classroom topics to large groups using brain-based approaches. I've seen hundreds of students gather in a gym, excited about complex problems they solved in every discipline, and faculty standing by, enjoying what their departments facilitated into action.

Drawing on the latest technological thinking, brain-based learning, and assessment approaches, brain-friendly initiatives provide e-strategies to diminish online frustrations and detail success strategies for faculty and students. Currently, I teach several graduate-level college classes online, have developed courses for secondary online classes, and have seen students and faculty work in teams with amazing results through e-exchanges. In addition, I belong to several faculty online discussion circles in which problems are shared whenever they arise. Support is only as far away as the next tap on the keyboard.

In roundtable sessions, faculty build online tools from what they already value in their traditional classes. Participants apply e-learning tactics that draw contributions from diverse individuals to guide the group to develop and teach brain-based lessons. Community comes from setting and sustaining a tone for interaction. My online students tell me they are surprised at how they get to meet new people in the online interactions, where two-footed questions stir up multiple responses on almost any topic that arises.

The online movement has opened wonderful windows for building online fireside chats among diverse thinkers. At places like the University of Phoenix Online and Touro University International, students are valued as team players in online communities, and their ideas are welcomed on each topic introduced. Because of this, students often tell me that they feel listened to, and because their ideas count, they are more motivated to develop new ideas as they learn and explore issues.

Because online roundtables focus on academic success within increasingly diverse learning communities, integration plays a key role in creating vibrant circles. This includes integration of technology tools and theories with students' or faculty experiences. Rather than focus on the technology operations alone, brain-based roundtables emphasize the *educative* tools that engage faculty's vast knowledge about their topics. In the best online programs, technicians lead the mechanistic components, and faculty lead in content areas.

As this new form of interactive education advances, faculty challenges will be to expand alternative approaches on an ongoing basis to include new practices compatible with the brain's capabilities, much like those practices illuminated in roundtable discussions. If we are to ensure that technology does not narrow people's approaches into one acceptable way only, we will want to encourage roundtables at their inception in order to bring together the best minds in an online community.

Online Roundtable Components

Online roundtables tend to cover four key areas:

1. Design and Develop Online Curriculum Maps

- Define multiple expectations.
- Follow a syllabus checklist.
- Build on benefits from diverse populations.
- Complete self-assessment quiz.

2. Create Teaching and Learning Spaces

- Create course calendar for daily posting.
- Identify barriers and bridges to good tone.
- Encourage multiple approaches.
- Complete self-assessment quiz.

3. Add Intelligence-Fair Assessment Tasks

- Build rubrics as guidelines.
- Motivate deeper understanding with two-footed questions.
- Plan ahead for less stress online.
- Complete self-assessment quiz.

4. Build Team Tools That Enhance Educative Goals

- Outline team skills that will be developed together.
- Provide diagnostic strategies to chart team progress.
- Create parallel routes to online goals and team voices.
- Complete self-assessment quiz.

Electronic Resource Bank

Faculty, online administrators, and students bring their individual interests and abilities to explore lessons together and apply brain-based tasks for online progress. Roundtables provide practical aid related to the educative components online, where multiple intelligence ideas foster online growth. You may find links and useful ideas at the following sites:

http://www.lib.nus.edu.sg/linus/98jan/etm98jan.html

http://www.newhorizons.org/trm_intr.html

http://www.mitaleadership.com

http://ss.uno.edu/SS/Theory/MultiIntelLks.html

http://sll.stanford.edu/projects/tomprof/home.html

http://proquest.umi.com/pqdweb?ReqType=301&UserId=IPAuto&Passwd=IPAuto&JSEnabled=1&TS=944491403

http://www.ksu.edu/biology/scholar/cooperative_learning_bibliography.htm

http://www.igs.net/~cmorris/spectrum.html

http://pzweb.harvard.edu/Research/ALPS.htm

Online Advantages for Secondary and College Students

Online is here to stay, and some secondary faculty are taking advantage of the opportunities to help build quality programs. If your roundtable decides to explore the online education world, you may want to investigate where your district is in electronic progress. You'll also want to look ahead to what your students' world will look like in the next few years. You will want to rethink how to prepare learners for the world they will enter economically, socially, and demographically. The Education Commission of the States predicts that secondary students will see an increased emphasis on highly personalized learning, student achievement, and school choice (*Future Trends Affecting Education,* retrieved March 4, 2004, from www.ecs.org/clearinghouse/13/27/1327.htm). The challenge is to implement innovative practices consistent with this emphasis.

Increasing disparity among schools that provide effective learning and those that do not is well documented. Effective learning is measured by results that prove higher motivation and achievement for most students. Regardless of how one scores the results, reports appear in public and government journals on a consistent basis to show which schools make it and which do not. Some schools claim that they need more money to address this problem. In roundtable programs, faculty address this problem by helping the learning community rethink learning for the changing needs of secondary and college students. Rather than demand more dollars from those who hold the already tightened public purse strings, roundtable communities propose to do more with what we already possess—students and faculty's incredible mental riches.

E-learning is used in varying degrees by the best schools. In an effort to stop pouring money into programs that no longer work in a changing community, one secondary school we work with decided to pay for what works well—online programs for disengaged teens. So far, the results are promising in pilot programs. In this case, the online opportunities created a new environment within which teachers could work with individuals who do not do well with lecture methods but do better with a more personalized learning setting. In discussion with the teachers who facilitate the program, I noted their use of brain-based innovations, which made the program work. These included personalized interactions and motivational tools to help students to achieve higher scores on standardized tests. Students worked from whatever place they entered the program so that they could progress to the next level effectively.

To learn online is to have access to effective tools that strengthen skills. Online programs like those highlighted in the article in Figure 7.9 add more opportunities for students to succeed in a variety of ways:

FIGURE 7.9   Article by Ellen Weber

Online pupils are on track to learn

Ellen Weber
Guest Essayist

I was glad to read that the Pittsford school district next fall will start offering online programs for high school students who need extra coursework, SAT preparation, or schoolwork during absences (story, Nov. 28).

Online secondary programs are booming in every state, with Keystone National High School, based in Pennsylvania, the largest, at over 130 e-courses. E-students can achieve higher educational goals, and still fit in sports, fun and work.

Furthermore, in the last year, Keystone students on average scored several points higher on SAT and ACT tests than did secondary students in schools across Pennsylvania. The online students also beat secondary students' scores nationally.

Still some protest, and online faculty tend to agree that a well-rounded education depends on faculty who can develop great courses and guide students to meet their goals.

After teaching dozens of online classes for adults and youths, I no longer believe the myth that face-to-face contact is preferable to computer settings. Learning is neither enhanced by live contact, in my experience, nor is it decreased in an online environment.

More and more students and teachers tend to agree that online classes offer new opportunities for individual growth. Team-building benefits also exist through e-learning that traditional classes often lack. It's been my experience that both teens and adults benefit more when online courses are developed with their input, and that, too, seems to be the case in Pittsford.

E-learning especially motivates students who are bored at school, since it draws on their abilities and offers frequent individualized feedback as well as self-assessment reviews. So higher test scores will result for these stu-

dents, and fewer should slip through the cracks. Schools interested in more involvement from parents or community members will likely build in interactive possibilities through Web or multimedia resources.

While e-learning is still in its early stages, we have a shot at ensuring more benefits and minimizing technical problems. To avoid making any U-turns back into classes that fail students, we'll want to support faculty as they learn new skills that convert live classes into software environments.

Students in the Pittsford program likely will learn cutting-edge skills they can take into any workplace.

Bravo! Jeffrey Cimmerer, the school district's director of technology, and his committee of 10 principals and teachers, received the school board's unanimous approval to roll out the first programs. Now it's time for public approval and help to build modern opportunities into valuable programs that our teens deserve.

Source: From the Rochester (NY) *Democrat and Chronicle,* Dec. 4, 2003, p. 19A. Used with permission.

Online initiatives provide opportunities to engage teachers as specialists in their fields. As noted in Figure 7.9, online learning opens a segue for brain-based practices that improve motivation and achievement. Currently, I am working with a group of e-faculty to increase the opportunities for students to use even more intelligences online. It is far more possible to explore and express knowledge in Gardner's eight ways of knowing than many realize. We find fewer answers in isolation than we do in supportive faculty circles.

EDUCATION REFORM AND FACULTY EMPOWERMENT

Sarason (1991) believes that faculty must be uniquely empowered for learning reform to succeed. He calls for increased authority for faculty in matters related to curriculum and administration. One way to do this is to create regular, rigorous roundtables and to support faculty who renew core curriculum approaches and implement the best brain-based tactics for measurable results in motivation and achievement. Fullan (1996) suggests that we go further by identifying strategies for faculty development that are consistent with goals of empowerment. In faculty roundtables, all population groups work together to create caring curriculum for diverse learning environments.

Faculty Reflection and MITA Roundtables

The influence of a five-pronged design for brain-friendly classes inspirits the language and directions you take in support circles, regardless of the disciplines or the culture you work within. At the outset, questions and dialogues abound around tables rather stand-and-deliver facts. Similarly, in preparing higher education lessons, start with significant questions. For example, on the topic of world hunger, the group might explore these questions: "Who are the world's hungry, and why should I care?" This two-footed question links questions to related content for deeper understanding of facts, figures, and cultural fusions to explore the lesson question "Who are the world's hungry?" The content questions are also linked to students' interests and abilities to create a lesson that draws from past knowledge and experiences to explore the question "Why should I care?"

At roundtables, faculty reflect on new knowledge gained and explore their learning process in order to improve future achievements. Through careful reflection they consider more effective ways to

- accommodate more student participation

- explore topics for deeper understanding

- motivate disengaged students

- integrate several fields of knowledge to solve complex, real-world problems

Creating College-Community Partnerships

Faculty roundtables welcome experts and novices, industrial workers, artists, and other scholars from diverse cultures through school-community partnerships. The wider community often contributes material resources or access to expertise through various field experiences. Industry offers tutoring and mentoring programs for students while providing state-of-the-art equipment, career shadowing opportunities, and leadership training (Bunting, 1994). Similarly, artists offer the keys to quality art, musicians provide segues into melody and composition, and athletes provide expertise about movement and kinesthetic strength. The best secondary schools offer ideas and academic models through which community expertise might be applied, mirrored, evaluated, and observed.

Critics of community involvement in high school fear that outsiders diminish secondary education. They cite examples of unfair and often purchased control of curriculum. These fears are well founded, since sometimes an outsider can dictate decisions rather than engage a community in rich dialogue. Similar fears exist whenever any one group silences another. This domination occurs at times even within some secondary education circles. High school and community partnerships work best when faculty, students, and community participants seek mutual opportunities to observe best practices and then create their own applications to learn or explore a particular topic. Industrial partnerships often lead to this point, particularly in the areas of technology advancement. Through shared decisions about escalated goals, more students will succeed at school.

Sharing Decision Making: Capitalizing on Human Intelligence

Through roundtable collaborations, faculty can shift from preparing teacher-centered materials, such as lectures, to ensuring student engagement. They move from teacher delivery or student memorizing to interactive inquiry and application of ideas. Through practical applications of human intelligence research and a commitment to welcome each person's interests and abilities in class, brain-based roundtables impact learning by

- providing a communication hub for change through ensuring that underrepresented populations participate actively in curriculum renewal

- creating interactive lessons that build bridges between learners and teachers across cultures, ages, and genders

- engaging faculty in step-by-step lesson topics of their choice and by posing significant lesson questions rather than presenting mere facts only, thereby using the human brain's optimum potential to achieve

- collaborating assessments for multiple approaches that demonstrate students' deep understanding of complex lesson topics

- improving educational climates through active use of students' intellectual domains and talents to answer significant lesson questions and increase test scores

- assisting faculty to reflect and adjust learning and teaching approaches in order to achieve higher learning standards

- creating a catalyst for change through partnerships with diverse faculty, both locally and globally

- improving brain-based resources through technology and online networking with diverse education partnerships

- modeling effective methods for curriculum renewal that include MITA's five-phase process and careful stewardship of center resources

Brain-based mentors work with faculty to

- research human intelligence as it impacts learning and teaching initiatives in secondary education classes

- create distance learning classes to provide MITA resources online for educators

- facilitate roundtables for regular professor-student interactions across diverse populations

- plan major conferences to introduce MITA renewal ideas and encourage collaboration

- construct curriculum materials with a variety of secondary and higher education learning communities

- teach leadership skills for those who wish to extend MITA ideas on home campuses

- create further brain-based research materials and resources for MITA curriculum.

CHANGING TO A BRAIN-FRIENDLY APPROACH

Renewal roundtables begin with two or more interested faculty. When institutions include Sarason's (1991) suggested empowerment of faculty, successful education reform results. It is important to create some time at every meeting so that obstacles are overcome and support is offered.

Faculty roundtables are ideal places to discuss how classrooms either prevent or foster genuine exploration and quality expression of knowledge. Classroom climates that prevent genuine understanding through MITA lessons sometimes view learning as what I call "empty bucket" and "shared ignorance" syndromes.

In the empty bucket syndrome, knowledge might include wordlists, phrases, concepts, problems, or insights spilled from one expert's head into a group of novices' heads, much as water spills from a vessel into empty buckets. This approach to knowledge assumes that to know is for students to gather facts or insights from lectures or textbooks and then to pour memorized facts back to satisfy standardized questions. It also assumes that teacher talk equals student learning.

The empty bucket syndrome, sometimes shaped largely by the British empirical tradition, is demonstrated in the "tabula rasa" concept of John Locke. Here teachers are viewed as fonts of knowledge, and students seen as "empty buckets." It is important to note that not that all lectures fit this description, since the best lecturers will offer opportunities for students to respond to core issues along the way.

One problem, with the empty bucket view and with lectures in general is that faculty fail to appreciate connecting ideas generated by students, peers, or community experts. In order to recognize students' unique giftedness and their ability to teach as well as learn from faculty, we need to encourage them to actively pose meaningful questions rather than simply write notes. Some faculty who shun small-group learning are participating in shared ignorance. These same faculty can tell horror stories resulting from cooperative learning circles done poorly.

The shared ignorance syndrome usually involves small groups learning together without clear guidance. In these cases, groups lack any clearly defined question to solve or significant product to create. Without criteria-based references or standardized benchmarks to achieve, key facts are sacrificed for reliance exclusively on experience or emotion. Some suggest that Dewey's emphasis on experience as a key to educational success has led teachers and professors to unbalanced preoccupation with experiences that shortchange learning achievement.

The shared ignorance syndrome, sometimes arising out of a false notion of Dewey's concept of student-centered discovery of knowledge, has contributed to a sort of anti-intellectualism that calls for disdaining facts and ignoring deeper understanding. While there are many books about the need for renewal in secondary education, far fewer books support teachers' efforts to link theory with practical classroom strategies that both improve students' opportunities for success and promote best practices for ongoing renewal. It's quite simple to convert complex theory into improved practice once you see a few illustrations and begin incrementally.

ENCOURAGING STUDENT PARTICIPATION

Mortimer Adler's goals for learning describe neither an empty bucket syndrome nor a shared ignorance syndrome. Adler demonstrates how students acquire knowledge. In his 1982 book, *The Paideia Proposal: An Education Manifesto*, Adler advocated

- the acquisition of organized knowledge

- the development of intellectual skills

- an enlarged understanding of ideas and values

Notice the innate influence of integration and ownership within these goals. Perhaps Adler's suggestions from 1982 can still help faculty today bring facts, figures, and discovery findings together in a more meaningful manner. My own research shows that there is still a ways to go in this regard.

Students interviewed over many years frequently detail their peers' excellent ideas. They also express regret that peers' ideas are rarely heard by faculty or welcomed in class. Peers are often described by their classmates as caring supporters who sometimes feel left out of high school or college class communications.

Faculty should not be surprised if some students take time before coming on board in their classes. Certainly, the two-footed questions highlighted in this book will help to open spaces for more input, and roundtables can help to break down barriers to student participation. Yet, for many students it's a matter of participation practice in a caring environment where mistakes are not viewed in diminishing ways. Just as caring partnerships take time and trust, relations among faculty and students require nurturing and patience. You will find that each time you invite students on board, more show up, and word soon gets around that you value their input.

It may break the ice and help students get involved through a revealing activity that identifies their own unique talents for learning. Since one often finds unique abilities hidden within activities in which people persist, do well, enjoy, or look forward to, faculty might discover that they can uncover the hidden potential of their students through surveys to identify these activities.

Some students express uncertainty about the value of their own contributions. Capabilities, whether in beginning or later stages, serve as tools for solving everyday problems or creating new ideas. MITA lessons or units may include musical, personal, artistic, communication, or mathematical problems, or they may be generated from everyday events. In most cases, complex problems warrant a wider array of students' multiple intelligences mix. Creative responses might include architectural ideas, songs, games, graphs, or communication ideas for posters or speeches. Make the central question at faculty circles, "How do we draw in passive or disengaged students?" and possibilities grow endless.

Start simply. I suggest you go back and select one or two ideas you liked as you reread Chapter 1. Start small and share the results so that others can help you to adjust for improvements. Many students have barely uttered a word in some high school classes, so it takes time and encouragement to help them express their ideas. Active involvement pays high dividends. Use the charts in each chapter to guide your students and let new ideas evolve for improving brain-based lessons each time you teach.

Teachers, students, and peers can increase communication not just with one another but also with the wider community. According to Eisner (1993), curriculum needs to reflect the "tasks they [students] will encounter in the world outside schools, not merely those limited to the schools themselves" (p. 226). Each circle will create a somewhat different road map for how they communicate for quality results. While my first roundtable group recognized the value of exchanging ideas with peers, for instance, our team was initially at a loss as to how to initiate such communication. It took time and discussion and many bridges between theory and practice in order to identify the map we wanted to follow.

A TIME TO APPLY, A TIME TO CREATE

Picasso was said to have done poorly in math class because every time he saw the number 4, he connected that 4 symbol to a picture of a nose in his mind. Because of his artistic talent, he simply enjoyed his creative connections, stopped problem solving, and drew wonderfully expressive faces around each 4.

Picasso's creation of faces from noses that should have been 4's would not have been tolerated by his teacher when he failed to complete his math assignments. I do not recommend that students ignore math and use their artistic talents. For both faculty and students, roundtables offer creative opportunities for enhanced understanding, as illustrated by the integration of learning theories and best practices you've encountered in this book. Benefits exist for faculty and for students while performance levels rise to excellent levels as a result of interactive circles.

Roundtable gatherings provide teachers and students both the depth of content and the scope of creativity required for lessons that engage them in deeper understanding. Artistic expression, hard facts, and people's capabilities come together in roundtables in the following ways:

• *Faculty* find support to adapt the amount of curriculum covered to the size and goals of each group; *students* find motivation to synthesize content in order to gain more understanding from the work.

• *Faculty* plan time allotments for learning exploration and assessment tasks; *students* learn to organize their time in order to complete the work.

• *Faculty* explore support opportunities; *students* enjoy increased personal assistance from faculty and peers.

• *Faculty* expand segues into new ideas through exploring rigorous possibilities; *students* capitalize on active learning that draws on their multiple intelligences.

• *Faculty* help one another to adapt the skill level of instruction, problem types, and rubrics; *students* adapt and find challenges along with support so they avoid frustration. Through adaptations, they link what they already know about lesson topics.

• *Faculty* design assessment tasks that express learners' proclivities for the topic and then adapt assessment approaches to suit outcomes they expect; *students* benefit from differentiated assessment that encourages them to reach higher standards through alternative tasks.

• *Faculty* use more mental acuity as they participate with others in similar pursuits; *students* participate actively with peers through well-crafted guidelines.

For both faculty and students, a well-facilitated circle with a common mission provides an extravagant idea cache, where support and encouragement help to generate excellent results. Regular gatherings are critical, and faculty will want to identify a theme and a facilitator for the next meeting each time they meet.

Remember: a onetime roundtable is much like a onetime seminar in that it stirs up innovation but lacks follow-up inspiration or support. Regular circles take planned determination to keep insights rolling in a positive direction. A rule of thumb is that for every good idea or good discussion, an excellent practice should form and follow. Once faculty make a decision to commit to peer interactions, all that is left is to jot the next date on the calendar, sketch an outline so that people will plan their contributions, and expect the group to remain on track for a wonderful adventure ahead.

In the appendix that follows, you will find further ideas to help you develop and create lesson and unit materials.

E-mail me if I can help your group further, at eweber1@frontiernet.net. Let us know at the MITA Renewal Center about your successes as roundtables evolve in your community. We'd love to hear your stories and to continue to share our discoveries. Daily research is adding new facts from neuroscience that will help improve teaching, learning, and assessment for those who consider new practices for brain-compatible benefits.

If you have become more interested in how certain practices capitalize more on students' brainpower than others, and if you have added those practices to your own roundtables, then this book did all I could have hoped! Your own roundtables will continue to generate best practices based on brain facts you uncover. As the book goes to press, new studies are emerging about the power of hope to release endorphins into the brain. The hormone dopamine can be tracked now by sophisticated brain scans that can chart the movement of molecules released in one's brain when hope is alive. *Anatomy of Hope,* a new book by Jerome Groopman (2003), a Harvard medical doctor, explores the powerful connection between hope and the release of chemical hormones into the brain that bring well-being, success, and life improvements.

Based on communications we receive at the center, more and more faculty are committed to implementing innovative practices garnered from these brain-based insights and practices such as those provided in this book. Hopefully, these pages have encouraged you to "go with your gut" and to convert brain facts into practices that will benefit you and your students. Start simply, with the few facts here, and soon others will be inspired by new fireworks from your own brain-based roundtables.

Assessment Task Planning with MITA

FIGURE A Project for English Unit

Unit Theme: Neruda's poetry and your poetry

Unit Question:
How might you see life through Neruda's eyes?

Unit Goals:
Publish your poem in a class collection as Neruda might write and publish it.

**Learning and
Assessment
Activities:**

Musical-rhythmic:
Select appropriate music to accompany your poem. Explain your choices. Or compose your poem into a song and present its melody, with music composed.

Visual-spatial: Create and photograph tableaux for 3 main themes in your poem. Title each photograph with a question that reveals the theme it depicts.

Verbal-linguistic: Type your poem in your favorite font. Read poem aloud into an audio- or videotape, using a musical background to enhance themes.

Mathematical-logical:
Sequence 5 main ideas from your poem. Create symbols for each. Then show how numbers inform your work. What might a mathematician ask?

Bodily-kinesthetic:
Choreograph and perform a dance on video. Your dance movements should illustrate the main points and themes of your poem.

Interpersonal: Create a crossword puzzle with a partner. Use words and ideas from your poem in each line. Exchange puzzles with another team and time your answers.

Intrapersonal: Read your poem aloud to yourself 2 or 3 times. Then show your main events or thoughts through Neruda's eyes, as he might have described them.

Naturalistic: Demonstrate recent research about natural problems or possibilities related to themes in your poem. Use nature to illustrate your responses.

Closure and Reflection:

Highlight 5 intelligences. Reflect on your responses to illustrate 5 intelligences. Create and submit a rubric with 6 key criteria highlighted. For instance, a grade could be based on spelling accuracy; similarity to Neruda's themes; having at least 14 lines, 3 nature themes; and original and creative ideas.

FIGURE B   Project for Social Studies Unit

Unit Theme: World cultures and our technology

Unit Question:

How has technology changed your culture?

Unit Goals:

Design a television show to show how technology changes culture.

Learning and Assessment Activities:

Musical-rhythmic: *Perform or play music from several cultures and show how technology could enhance or prevent further cultural understandings.*

Visual-spatial: *Create a symbol or visual model to represent each culture in your class. Gather feedback from members of each culture and edit your designs.*

Verbal-linguistic: *Create and facilitate a debate about the problems and possibilities of technology to enhance cultural advancement during the next decade.*

Mathematical-logical: *Solve cultural problems using technology-related solutions. Defend your choices and show how they increase cultural exchanges.*

Bodily-kinesthetic: *Simulate cultural differences concerning technology in a skit or dance, mime, or gymnastic routine.*

Interpersonal: *Interview a technology expert and a person who dislikes technology and compare their responses to identical questions about technology.*

Intrapersonal: *Reflect on your culture and show similarities and differences to other cultures represented in your classmates.*

Naturalistic: *Demonstrate how nature and technology work together or at odds in different cultures. Suggest solutions to problems identified.*

Closure and Reflection:

Highlight at least 5 intelligences on a mock TV show that responds to the main project question here. Create and submit a rubric for 6 criteria expected in each mock TV presentation. Check these criteria with the teacher.

FIGURE C Project for Science Unit

Unit Theme: How can we improve water near my home?

Unit Question:
How can a community identify river quality problems and enhance clean water?

Unit Goals:
Create a river quality portfolio to present to community and government officials.

**Learning and
Assessment
Activities:**

Verbal-linguistic: Write a speech to inspire any group to clean up rivers and protect water quality in their communities. Present the speech and invite feedback.

Interpersonal: Interview several experts concerning rivers in your area. Lay out several cooperative tasks that would resolve problems expressed.

Musical-rhythmic: Create musical representations to make your points about river quality problems and possibilities in your area. Present your findings and solutions.

Mathematical-logical: Describe a sequential plan for data collection and analysis for a group of researchers who want to identify water quality problems and create solutions.

Intrapersonal: Write daily journals for 10 days and in your writing identify moral decisions critical to water quality in rivers near your home. Suggest plans for individuals.

Visual-spatial: Design a poster or artistic display to help people see river quality problems and possibilities. Use few words and many symbols or designs.

Bodily-kinesthetic: Construct a physical mock-up to show your solutions to water quality problems. Defend your solutions and describe how builders can help.

Naturalistic: Use nature to show the problems and possibilities of water quality in your area. Suggest how naturalists can help solve problems and ensure quality.

Closure and Reflection:

Highlight 8 intelligences in your portfolios. Create and submit rubrics for 6 criteria expected in each portfolio inclusion. Check criteria with teacher.

FIGURE D   Addition to Science Lesson Project

To further elaborate the science project in Figure C, you and your students can select a committee of eight to create a proactive plan to explore water quality in rivers near students' home.

Statement of Objective

A wonderful new river quality plan will be discussed on video to present to government leaders and the public in your area. Part of the plan requires research and action from different members of your community. You have been asked to draw people together and to participate yourself in a roundtable discussion to develop guidelines that ensure river quality. Together, your team will create a portfolio to defend your river quality plan for this community. Show why your plan will work to keep rivers clean and convince any audience that you have created a plan that includes their best interests.

Committee Roles

Members in your committee should include students in each of the following roles:

1. You are a **secondary science teacher,** and your job is to identify an excellent question to explore for research by the team. Identify the question that most needs to be researched by this committee and describe a detailed plan for gathering information and conducting research. Sequence the steps and procedures of your plan and convince the team that your plan will benefit all members and increase river water quality, if followed. (mathematical inquiry)

2. You are an **environmental leader** and deeply concerned that nature has been neglected in your area for big business. Money has been given priority over river conservation. You see apathy and feel concerned that older members of the community have no idea how endangered rivers have become. Using nature research, show one strategy for solving the question posed and defend your conclusions. (spatial inquiry)

3. You are a **local musician** interested in music's ability to create changed attitudes about river quality and its importance to survival of any community. Music is your tool to respond to the question, and you create music to present to a local TV station, after trying your creation out on this committee. Your lyrics and sound distinctions should help to support your main theme about river quality problems and possibilities in your area. (musical inquiry)

4. You are an **artist** in this community and make your case for river quality in visual representations. You might develop graphs, geometric designs, diagrams, artistic displays, maps, sculpturing, or other visual communications to make your points clear. Your art will be displayed in a local museum and should therefore be developed in final, polished form and presented to the group for their discussion. (visual inquiry)

5. You are a **wise elder and leader** in your community. You write a daily journal about river problems and possibilities and often refer to the moral judgments that contribute to great quality in rivers. You advocate self-management and show a plan where people can personally contribute to finer water quality in rivers. (intrapersonal inquiry)

6. You are a **politician,** and you suggest a strategy for team work to ensure river quality. You include intercultural groups and show how you can use river quality issues to draw diverse groups together. You lay out several cooperative tasks for a team to help solve problems identified in river conservation. Then you facilitate pair sharing on this committee to develop lasting water quality with team commitment after this committee dissolves. You address fears and concerns of people in area. (interpersonal inquiry)

7. You are a **gymnast and builder,** and you care about constructing physical projects to help river quality as new buildings develop in river areas. You are tired of words alone and want more action from concerned citizens and builders who can create a physical structure to ensure river quality. Create a mock-up of the structure you create and present it to the committee for their approval. (bodily-kinesthetic inquiry)

8. You are a **speaker and writer,** and you prepare and deliver a brief speech that will inspire any audience to clean up rivers and protect water quality. Your speech will be used in a media report to the community about current river quality, problems estimated, research indications, and a plan for new possibilities to preserve water quality in future. (linguistic inquiry).

Procedure

Each participant presents findings and solutions on video or before a live audience. After the presentations, the materials are gathered into a professional portfolio and presented to a local government official in order to defend and illustrate river quality in your area. Make sure you identify problems and suggest possible solutions in clear illustrations that highlight multiple perspectives

FIGURE E   Project for Mathematics Unit

Unit Theme: How graphs and wars affect your life

Unit Question:

How could graphs help you win or lose a war?

Unit Goals:

Create graphs to show government leaders the effects of war and peace.

Learning and Assessment Activities:

Musical-rhythmic: *Create sound effects to enhance your graphic display about a war currently taking place that involves your country.*

Visual-spatial: *Exhibit diverse graphs to show and defend war or peace. Your display should be original and artistic as well as easily understood by viewers.*

Verbal-linguistic: *Summarize a graphic demonstration of wars in your own words, for a speech a senator might bring to the president to defend or prevent a war in the future.*

Mathematical-logical: *Solve 3 war or peace problems using charts to explain and illustrate your solutions. Analyze data from both sides of the issue.*

Bodily-kinesthetic: *Build a graph with materials other than paper and pencil and show how graphs can change outcomes for war or peace.*

Interpersonal: *Share and discuss you graphs as they represent war and peace concerns. Come to a consensus with a peer about graph's uses for ensuring future peace.*

Intrapersonal: *Reflect and draw conclusions about how graphs can create or diminish good moral choices about war and lead to peaceful decisions.*

Naturalistic: *Use graphs to show naturalistic concerns during war and peace. How might these be represented by an environmental expert?*

Closure and Reflection:

Highlight at least 5 intelligences in your presentation to government leaders. Get feedback from leaders in your community and videotape their responses to your graphs and displays for war or peace.

FIGURE F MITA Assessment Tasks for Additional Topics

Similar tasks to those that follow can be adapted to your lesson topics to ensure that students draw from multiple domains to express knowledge. Note that learning and assessment tasks are at times similar or even the same, in some cases. Using the chart provided in Figure G, have students list intelligences used and assessed during each project. For instance, assessment tasks for a unit about the Arctic might include the following:

Verbal-Linguistic Demonstration

- Create a story.
- Write a research paper.
- Interview an expert.
- Interpret a chapter of text.
- Write a poem.
- Design a book of comparisons.
- Lecture peers.
- Read chorally.

Mathematical-Logical Demonstration

- Graph climate and temperature changes.
- Design a Website using scientific principles, laws, and theorems.
- Interview a scientist.
- Outline a chapter of text.
- Create a business proposal for an Arctic enterprise.
- Create schedules.
- Create hidden messages.
- Use values to find solutions.

Visual-Spatial Demonstration

- Create a mock-up.
- Design a building to survive permafrost.
- Paint.
- Draw.
- Build 3-D objects.
- Create posters to illustrate two sides of an issue.
- Display bulletin boards.
- Create a software program.

Bodily-Kinesthetic Demonstration

- Choreograph a dance.
- Create a tableau.
- Build MITA learning centers.
- Travel to museums.
- Design outdoor learning site.
- Produce a play.
- Use body language.
- Re-create Arctic games and sports.

Musical-Rhythmic Demonstration

- Create a melody.
- Integrate music and learning.
- Demonstrate musical vibrations.
- Interpret Arctic life through music.
- Write a song.
- Create an Arctic music video.
- Prepare musical backgrounds.
- Perform solos, duets, or trios.

Interpersonal Demonstration

- Create a shared story.
- Interview peers.
- Team teach a concept.
- Collaborate with a teacher.
- Describe Arctic characters.
- Illustrate ethical choices of Arctic leaders.
- Create an Arctic marketing scheme.
- Proofread a peer's essay.

Intrapersonal Demonstration

- Create a journal from perspective of an Inuit your age.
- Write personal reflections on an Arctic issue.
- Illustrate your personal ethics on a controversial topic.
- Write personal stories.
- Design personal portfolio of Arctic projects.
- Illustrate personal goal-setting strategies.
- Create an Inuit scrapbook.
- Publish a personal book.

Naturalistic Demonstration

- Compare and contrast the Arctic environment to your own.
- Demonstrate research about natural Arctic problems.
- Complete experiments from nature.
- Communicate with Arctic environmental specialists over the Internet.
- Illustrate natural Arctic phenomena.
- Sort and categorize information from geographic sites.
- Write a naturalistic response to a common climactic problem.
- Compare Arctic hunting patterns today with the past.

FIGURE G   Form for Student MITA Self-Assessment

Intelligences:	Ways each intelligence was used to respond:
Verbal-linguistic	
Bodily-kinesthetic	
Interpersonal	
Intrapersonal	
Mathematical-logical	
Musical-rhythmic	
Naturalistic	
Visual-spatial	

FIGURE H   Form for Planning MITA Project Tasks and Assessment

Title:

Question:

Goals:

**Learning and
Assessment
Activities:**

| Verbal-linguistic: | Interpersonal: |

Musical-rhythmic:

| Mathematical-logical: | Intrapersonal: |

Visual-spatial:

| Bodily-kinesthetic:. | Naturalistic: |

Closure and Reflection:

Bibliography

Adler, M. (1982). *The Paideia proposal: An education manifesto.* New York: Macmillan.

Anderson, C. S. (1982). The search for school climate: A review of the research. *Review of Educational Research, 52,* 368–420.

Bateson, M. C. (1990). *Composing a life: Life as a work in progress—the improvisations of five extraordinary women.* New York: Penguin.

Brown, Rexford G. (1991). *Schools of thought: How the politics of literacy shape thinking in the classroom.* San Francisco: Jossey Bass.

Brownell, H. H., Michel, D., Powelson, J., & Gardner, H. (1983). Surprise but not coherence: Sensitivity to verbal humor in right-hemisphere patients. *Brain and Language, 18*(1), 20–27.

Bruner, J. (1979). After John Dewey, what? In *On knowing: Essay for the left hand.* Boston, MA: Harvard University Press.

Bunting, C. (1987). Educational purpose and the new curricula. *NASSP Bulletin, 71,* 119–125.

Bunting, C. (1994). Building a school-industrial partnership. *Middle School Journal, 25*(15), 43–45.

Burgess, C. (1984). Public schooling, a historical perspective. *Childhood Education, 61,* 91–98.

Burgess, C. (1985). Models of the learner. *Educational Researcher, 23,* 5–8.

Campbell, B., Campbell, L., & Dickinson, D. (1992). *Teaching and learning through multiple intelligences.* Seattle, WA: New Horizons for Learning.

Campbell, D. (2001). *The Mozart effect: Tapping the power of music to heal the body, strengthen the mind, and unlock the creative spirit.* New York: Random House.

Cuban, L. (1990). A fundamental puzzle of school reform. In A. Lieberman (Ed.), *Schools as collaborative cultures: Creating the future now* (pp. 71–77). New York: Falmer Press.

Doyle, W. (1983). Academic work. *Review of Education Research, 53,* 159–199.

Eisner, E. W. (1985). On the uses of educational criticism for evaluating classroom life. *Teachers' College Record, 78,* 345–358.

Eisner, E. W. (1993). Reshaping assessment in education: Some criteria in search of practice. *Journal of Curriculum Studies, 25*(3), 219–233.

Emerson, R. W. (1849/1992). *The American scholar: The selected writings of Ralph Waldo Emerson.* New York: Random House.

Freire, P. (2000). *Pedagogy of the oppressed.* London: Continuum.

Fullan, M. (1996). Turning systemic thinking on its head. *Phi Delta Kappan, 77*(6), 420–423.

Gardner, H. (1991). *The unschooled mind.* New York: Basic Books.

Goleman, D. (1995). *Emotional intelligence: Why it can matter more than IQ.* New York: Bantam.

Goodlad, J. (1997). *In praise of education.* New York: Teachers College Press

Goodman, K., Goodman, Y., & Hood, W. (Eds.). (1989). *The whole language evaluation book.* Toronto: Irwin.

Greene, M. (1991). Texts and margins. *Harvard Educational Review, 61*(1), 27–39.

Groopman, J. (2003). *Anatomy of hope.* New York: Random House.

Hamm, C. (1989). *Philosophical issues in education: An introduction.* New York: Falmer Press.

Hargreaves, A., & Fullan, M. (Eds.). (1992). *Understanding teacher development.* New York: Teachers College Press.

Hart, L. (1983). *Human brain and human learning.* New York: Basic Books.

Higher Education Research Institute, UCLA. (2000). "Report: Students Fret over College Bills, Boredom of Senior Year." Retrieved from www.amarillonet.com.

Hoerr, T. (2000). *Becoming a multiple intelligence school.* Alexandria, VA: Association for Supervision and Curriculum Development.

Jacobs, H. H. (1989). *Interdisciplinary curriculum: Design and implementation.* Alexandria, VA: Association for Supervision and Curriculum Development.

Jensen, Eric. (1998). *Teaching with the brain in mind.* Alexandria, VA: Association for Supervision and Curriculum Development.

Kasten, W., & Clarke, B. (1993). *The multi-age classroom: A family of learners.* Katonah, NY: Owen.

Kovalik, S. (1994). *ITI: The model—integrated thematic instruction.* Kent, WA: Books for Educators.

Lieberman, A. (1992). The meaning of scholarly activity and the building of community. *Educational Researcher,* Aug.–Sept., 5–12.

Lieberman, A., & Miller, L. (1990). Restructuring schools: What matters and what works. *Phi Delta Kappan, 71,* 759–764.

Lim-Alparaque, I. (1990). Making practical notions of pedagogical theorizing. In R. Evans, A. Winning, & M. van Manen (Eds.), *Reflections on pedagogy and method* (pp. 88–103). Alberta: Banff School of Fine Arts.

Lucas, C. (1996). *Crisis in the academy: Rethinking higher education in America.* London: Macmillan.

National Commission on Excellence in Education. (1983). *A nation at risk.* Washington, DC: U.S. Department of Education.

Peck, S. (1988). *The different drum: Community making and peace.* Toronto: Simon & Schuster.

Perkinson, H. (1987). *Two hundred years of educational thought.* New York: University Press of America.

Ravitch, D. (1983). *The troubled crusade.* New York: Basic Books.

Sarason, S. B. (1991). *The predictable future of educational reform.* San Francisco: Jossey-Bass.

Shekerjian, D. (1990). *Uncommon genius: How great ideas are born.* New York: Penguin Books.

Sizer, T. R. (1992). *Horace's school: Redesigning the American high school.* Boston: Jones & Bartlett.

Smagorinsky, P. (1992). *Expressions: MI intelligences in the English class.* Urbana, IL: National Council of Teachers of English.

Spady, W., & Marshall, K. (1991). Beyond traditional outcome-based education. *Educational Leadership, 49*(2), 67–72.

Sternberg, R. J., and Gardner, H. (1991). Creating creative minds. *Phi Delta Kappan,* Apr., 608–614.

Sullivan, C. (2001). *Body knows.* New York: Hay House.

Swartz, R. (1976). Mistakes as an important part of the learning process. *High School Journal, 59*(6), 246–257.

Travers, P. L. (1985). On unknowing. *Parabola: Myth and the Quest for Meaning, 10*(3), 76–79.

Van Manen, M. (1990). *Researching lived experience: Human science for an action sensitive pedagogy.* London: Althouse Press.

Villa, R. A., & Thousand, J. S. (1992). Restructuring public school systems: Strategies for organizational change and progress. In R. A. Villa, J. S. Thousand, W. Stainback, & S. Stainback (Eds.), *Restructuring for caring and effective education: An administrative guide to creating heterogeneous schools* (pp. 109–140). Baltimore: Brookes.

Vygotsky, L. S. (1978). *Mind in society: The development of higher mental processes.* Cambridge, MA: Harvard University Press. (Original works published 1930, 1933, 1935.)

Vygotsky, L. S. (1986). *Thought and language.* (A. Kozulin, Trans.). Cambridge, MA: MIT Press. (Original work published 1934.)

Weber, E. (1992). Curriculum for success. *On the Beam, 12*(3), 4–5.

Weber, E. (1995). *Creative learning from inside out.* Vancouver, BC: EduServ.

Weber, E. (1999). *Student assessment that works: A practical approach.* Needham Heights, MA: Allyn and Bacon.

Weber, E. (2000). Five phases to problem-based learning: MITA model for redesigned higher education classes. In T. O. Seng, P. Little, H. S. Yin, & J. Conway (Eds.), *Problem-based learning: Educational innovation across disciplines* (pp. 65–76). Singapore: Temasek Center for Problem-Based Learning.

Whitehead, A. (1959). *The aims of education and other essays.* New York: Macmillan.

Index

Note: f indicates a figure, and t indicates a table.